Realms of Legal Interpretation

Realms of Legal Interpretation

Core Elements and Critical Variations

KENT GREENAWALT

OXFORD
UNIVERSITY PRESS

OXFORD
UNIVERSITY PRESS

Oxford University Press is a department of the University of Oxford. It furthers the University's objective of excellence in research, scholarship, and education by publishing worldwide. Oxford is a registered trade mark of Oxford University Press in the UK and certain other countries.

Published in the United States of America by Oxford University Press
198 Madison Avenue, New York, NY 10016, United States of America.

CIP data is on file at the Library of Congress
ISBN 978-0-19-088286-0

To those in our world who care for others

CONTENTS

ACKNOWLEDGMENTS

In terms of scholarly assistance, I wish to acknowledge all those who have helped me with earlier works, which are the main sources on which this book is based. In respect to research assistance, Daniel Sack, careful and thorough, has been my primary helper here. Michael Donaldson has also given significant help. Katherine Bobbitt, as with other projects, has been key to translating my ideas, with edits, into effective communication.

Realms of Legal Interpretation

Introduction

This book considers the range of circumstances in which courts must decide what is legally forbidden or authorized. In none of the domains discussed does there exist an agreement regarding all the details of the methods United States judges should employ or how judges should state what moves them to a decision. Plainly, which approaches make good sense differs depending upon which issues are at stake. For example, the appropriate way to interpret the free speech clause of the Constitution differs from how a person's will should be understood. In this book, I do indicate my views about what judges might sensibly do in various areas, but that is not my main purpose. My main purposes are to provide for readers who are not experts with regard to legal interpretation a brief summary of what judges do take into account and how judges formulate their decisions; to explain how the various domains of law reasonably lead to different kinds of approaches, even when all domains involve forms of texts with legal authority; and to show how various categorizations that seem decisive are not really so. A primary objective is to reach non-lawyers and lawyers whose main concerns lie elsewhere. But some of the chapters engage in discussions that may also benefit readers who are expert lawyers or experts in other domains of interpretation. Chapter 4, on other countries, provides us with bases for comparison, including evaluations of aspects of our own system. Chapter 5, on other forms of interpretation, including religious and literary interpretation, may help us, and those who concentrate on those forms of interpretation, understand how such forms resemble and differ from what judges do with legal sources. Chapter 3's concentration on categorization, as well as other chapters, helps to reveal how various relevant categories can help us to understand what judges and others are doing. Nevertheless, these categories cannot by themselves produce correct answers as to how difficult cases should be decided. Even within the first two chapters on basic interpretive practices, readers will find a good bit of analysis and observation that bears on what we should perceive as realistic and desirable practices, as compared with some simplistic and misleading rhetoric.

Various categorizations, such as "applying the law" as contrasted with "making the law," can help us to understand existing and desirable judicial practices. But, like most categorizations that bear on our lives, these are hardly precise. Instead, they are often fuzzy at the edges. When we think about whether a particular practice is desirable, we need to focus on its actual benefits and drawbacks, not on exactly what category covers it. In this respect, I also believe that sophisticated theories about what is "law," such as legal positivism versus some modern versions of natural law, are not very helpful. A reader who engages with the entire book will come away with a more modest view about the genuine importance of line drawing for categories bearing on legal interpretation than many legal scholars have asserted.

I shall first outline the various domains that are covered. I then turn to what factors may influence judicial understanding. I briefly explain why non-legal analogues can be revealing about what may count and why. The summary following these remarks focuses on what we should see as the role of judges and on what the process of "interpretation" arguably includes and does not include. The following chapters delve into all these subjects in greater detail, and do so in a way that aims to be accessible to all interested readers.

It is worth noting how this endeavor relates to my prior work, of which some readers may be aware. In addition to various articles, from 2010 to 2015 I authored three books on legal interpretation: *Legal Interpretation, Perspectives from Other Disciplines and Private Texts; Statutory and Common Law Interpretation*; and *Interpreting the Constitution*. Each of these focuses mainly on particular domains. These books do make some comparisons between different subjects, so what I undertake here is not completely novel. But much in this book is not derivable from the earlier ones, and I try here to present in a clear and straightforward way ideas that one might gather from the prior books only by reading and digesting more than 1,200 pages.

Legal norms may forbid, require, or authorize behavior; and, of course, some norms may do more than one of these. The law of contracts, for example, informs people how to enter into agreements that will bind both sides, and their agreement results in a legal requirement of how they should behave. When we turn to government officials, the legal provisions grant authority for legislators and executive officials to set standards for citizens, and they give judges the authority to decide disputes by applying and interpreting governing standards. The law also sets the methods by which these officials are chosen.

Although many legal requirements are directly set by those who are officials, such as legislators and executive officers, much of what is demanded by law comes from choices of private citizens, such as wills and contracts. The book's treatment of privately created legal requirements covers these two domains, as well as grants of benefits over time in trusts that can lead to "cy-pres." Officially created standards include statutes, administrative regulations, constitutional provisions, and rules made by courts themselves as parts of the common law or as products of judicial treatment of other binding provisions, such as the Constitution's First Amendment.

What are the factors that do and should count in figuring out what is legally required? I shall note two matters that are very important. Although with some frequency, individuals may be unaware of legal requirements that relate to their behavior, people generally comply with legal restraints without judicial involvement. If the language of a legal requirement clearly suggests a particular result, when the language fits the intentions of those who formulated the requirement, and when the consequence of the result is just and makes practical sense, that application is how private citizens, enforcement officials, and judges will understand it.

Problems arise only when these factors either do not yield clear answers, or obviously (or arguably) do not fit together and therefore conflict in a sense. Should private citizens, executive officials, and judges all treat those situations the same way? For example, what should judges and others do if the text of a statute does not carry out what appears to be the intentions of the legislators, or if people have obviously omitted something they intended from a will or contract, or have made an outright mistake in what they have written? Those discerning what is required must then consider how much weight to give to the text and how much to actual or likely intentions. If one focuses on what the text means, one question to consider is what readers should count—ordinary people or those who are expert or highly sophisticated? For intentions, and also texts, how far can overall purposes outweigh specific applications? In both domains, should the exclusive or main focus be on original understanding, or should judges and others also take account of changing conditions since the standard was set?

Considering non-legal analogues, such as ordinary instructions and agreements without legal force, can be enlightening for a number of reasons. The first is that these are parts of our everyday lives. How informal instructions should fit with what we think we and others should do is a part of our common experiences. It helps us to think about how the law does, or should, differ here. Of course, to be clear, no one should assume that the treatment of informal instructions fits directly with the law. There are crucial differences.

Can we come up with decisive answers to all the questions about how we should react to non-legal instructions if the semantic content misfits with broader intentions, or circumstances have changed significantly? If, as I shall urge, this is genuinely impossible for most of us, how, if at all, is the law critically different? Reasoning by analogy from outcomes that are clearly settled or obviously right can work both within the law and with informal relations, but the law has settled outcomes in the common law and judicial decisions that are often the source of legal analogy. If we put aside things such as religious convictions, we see that these authoritative starting points do not exist informally. More modestly, is it at least very important for judges to try to rely upon and to formulate clear criteria for reaching decisions?

When we reflect on our personal, non-legal situations, we can in some respects better evaluate what is feasible for the law, although we must also perceive important differences. A key related factor here is one I have already mentioned: most legal requirements are voluntarily carried out by individuals subject to them. For such people, life may be simpler if the ways in which they assess these requirements are not so different from how they would understand and perform other, non-legal responsibilities.

Two theoretical questions about what judges do are (1) whether and when they should see themselves as "faithful agents" or independent actors, and (2) what constitutes "interpretation" as contrasted with, or related to, simple "application" and "construction" or "reformulation." Of course, in the vast majority of cases in which judges rule on what is the "law," they are acting as faithful agents in the separation of powers by carrying out the will of the legislature, or by fulfilling what the makers of contracts designed. But in some more difficult cases, such as the significance of changing conditions, their proper role is more debatable. I believe it is important here to focus directly on what practices by judges are desirable, not whether such practices can best be characterized as those of faithful agency or independence.

The question of what counts as "interpretation" and what involves extending beyond "interpretation" to a form of judicial construction is far from simple. I shall explore this to some degree in the chapters that follow, but two points here are very important. Like most other categories, the term "interpretation" does not have precise edges; people can reasonably disagree over whether some exercise is, or is not, really interpretation. Partly for this reason, it is unproductive to put huge emphasis on whether some exercise by judges extends beyond "interpretation." Although different uses of the term often come into play in conflicting analyses of what judges do and might do, the crucial questions concern what individuals, officials, and judges *should do* under the law. This should not depend directly on just how wide one sees "interpretation" as reaching. Another term that can involve somewhat different forms is "meaning" itself; it can sometimes be misleading to refer to "*the* meaning" as though only one is possible. As with "faithful agents," and "meaning," the focus on judicial practice should be on what makes sense in our system for judges to do, not whether that exercise qualifies as "interpretation" or extends to something further.

A point worth noting in this introduction is that the court on which a judge sits can sometimes matter greatly. There is a huge amount of focus on the United States Supreme Court. Lower court judges may need to adopt somewhat different approaches to certain matters than Supreme Court justices. Notably, they have much less basis to overturn Supreme Court precedents. When one thinks about what judges should do, being clear about which judges one is focusing on can be very important.

Our next two chapters deal with basic issues about legal interpretation. The first asks about the relevant importance of textual meaning and drafters' intentions, how they may be determined by judges, and how far sensible answers to these questions depend on the kinds of documents involved. It involves inquiries about the relevant significance of the language of specific provisions in relation to broader purposes, and asks how far judges should aim to be candid about all they take into account. The second chapter focuses on changes over time of social organizations and on accompanying changes in values, questions most directly relevant for open-ended constitutional provisions, such as an equal protection clause, whose coverage may broaden or narrow as society evolves. The third chapter tackles a more complex topic: How can various categorizations, such as "faithful agent" or "not making law" be understood, and how far can these categories carry us in determining what judges do, and should do? As I have noted, for hard cases I am substantially skeptical about any yielding of decisive answers here.

The fourth chapter makes references to other legal systems, explaining why processes can matter, whether they do not make nearly as much difference as may appear linguistically, and whether arguable strengths in one system are likely to yield genuine flaws in another. The fifth chapter looks at other disciplines. Such comparisons can yield important insights about why things matter, but can also reveal fundamental dissimilarities in what the aims are of various forms of interpretation. In both these last chapters, I believe one can learn much that is enlightening from other forms, but they do not tell us in any detail how judges should behave.

A related question to many other questions in the book is how far judges attempt to be candid about all they do and whether they should aim to be more candid about the bases for their decisions and what legal standards require. These are complicated questions that we shall touch upon in various contexts.

Should judges state everything on which they rely and fully disclose what they see as the force of competing considerations? That question concerns the degree to which judges should reveal that the accepted legal standards themselves do not always provide clear answers, and that they must rely on other assessments of a practical or moral sort. Of course, any aspiration of complete candor is significantly curtailed by the place of majority opinions, since in difficult cases these often include judges who actually see things somewhat differently.

With this introduction, we shall now turn to a closer examination of differences in standards of interpretation and some troubling questions these raise.

1

Text or Intent, or Both

A controversial subject in many domains of legal standards is how much weight to give the text itself in relation to the intentions of those who formulated it or whose agreement, such as legislators voting, brought the text's standards into actual effect. If the emphasis is on the text, then what counts is the understanding of readers. The intentions concern what was in the minds, and may have been expressed, by those who brought the standards into being. A claim by some "traditionalists" concerning statutory and constitutional interpretation is that subjective intentions are effectively irrelevant, at least as far as judicial interpretation is concerned. A dominant theme of this chapter is that this position does not make sense from an intrinsic conceptual point of view. It is plausible only insofar as inquiries about intent are effectively impossible, too costly, or likely to be badly misguided, whether self-consciously or not. A claim of impossibility may rest on the assumption that no relevant intent exists, for instance, with regard to provisions in complex statutes or contracts, or that in a great many situations judges are incapable of discerning an intent that would matter. In the chapters to follow, I will explore some of these nuances. Here, I start with when and why intentions are intrinsically relevant. I shall subsequently look at the significance of justice, public policy, and changed circumstances.

Intentions may seem important if the relevant text is indecisive about a possible application or is thought to be at odds with likely intentions. A text itself may be indecisive in three different ways. One way is that its standard is open-ended and does not itself determine many possible applications. For example, whether a punishment is "cruel and unusual," under the Eighth Amendment to the federal constitution, is often not going to be settled by some simple application of that language without any other evaluation. A second possibility is that the semantic language may definitely point in one direction or another, but common understandings of uses of that language may be more complicated. A third possibility is that the textual language may be fairly specific, but an arguable application may lie at the edges; or two parts of the specific language may seem in conflict with each other. A fourth situation of uncertainty, one not involving textual indecisiveness, is when the text appears clearly applicable in a certain reasonable way, but the claim is made that this application did not fit with the actual intentions of those who counted, such as the makers of a contract. Beyond actual intentions that indicate what situations creators actually considered, people may ask about hypothetical intentions—what the creators would have concluded if this circumstance had occurred to them.

Those receiving instructions generally understand what speakers say or writers write in accord with what they take as the intentions of those telling them what to do. Suppose a ten-year-old child has done something wrong and her father says, "Go to your room for an hour and do not come out for any reason." After thirty minutes, lightning strikes through an open window and furniture catches on fire. A perceptive daughter will leave the room to protect herself and tell the parents what has happened. If she asks herself about her father's intentions, she realizes that "not for any reason" does not typically include the most powerful conceivable reasons, such as saving one's life. If the daughter instead simply stayed in the room until her father realized a fire had broken out, came into the room, and removed her, we can imagine the following conversation: Dad: "Why didn't you come out when the fire started?"; Daughter: "You told me not to do so for any reason"; Dad: "This sort of reason was not what I meant." A somewhat similar example would be a basketball coach telling his players not to shoot when they have the ball and lead by three points with only fifteen seconds left in the game. The players may realize that the coach does not mean to exclude an extremely easy shot that a player always makes.

I once had a personal experience that involved the possible application of a legal standard that was somewhat similar. I was stopped for driving too fast, and effectively instructed to pull over and park on the side of a street that said "No Parking. I answered honestly to the policeman about my speed; he was generous and gave me a modest parking ticket instead of a speeding ticket. Now, when the law authorizes a sign that says "No Parking," no one would suppose it actually applies if the only reason you are parking there is because a police officer has directed you to do so. *If* I had chosen to litigate the parking ticket itself, I would probably have succeeded.

Suppose a city adopts an ordinance that bars "sleeping" in its railroad stations, and this prohibition is posted in the stations. Will a passenger whose train has been delayed for two hours late in the evening believe he is violating the ordinance if he takes a brief nap while sitting and waiting for his train? Here much will depend on what publicity, if any, has accompanied the enactment. If the obvious concern has been that poor, homeless people have been using the stations as their bedrooms, disconcerting regular passengers, then the passenger here will not suppose that a one-hour nap while sitting counts as forbidden "sleeping." But imagine that the underlying background is different. Suppose that homeless residents are not using the stations to sleep. Instead, late at night, passengers who fall asleep while waiting are being robbed. If these robberies have been well publicized as the basis for the rule, a passenger will assume he should try hard to stay awake. How a passenger understands the words "No sleeping" will be closely related to what he understands as the objectives of those who adopted the rule. How one grasps such a text is related to what one takes as the intentions of the adopters.

In June 2017, we were provided with an interesting example of what a word issued by a higher authority entailed for his subordinates. President Donald Trump conveyed his "hope" to James Comey that the investigation of Michael Flynn would be curtailed.[1] "I hope" can be expressed in all sorts of ways. Many simply reflect hopes for a particular outcome, such as your son's team winning a game, but without any effort to influence behavior. On the other hand, if one makes clear he will otherwise impose a negative consequence, "I hope you will do x" can indicate what is needed to avoid that consequence. If a person in power tells a subordinate what he hopes the subordinate will do, he may or may not make clear what will happen if the hope is not satisfied. The subordinate may believe, as did Comey, that he is getting an implicit instruction; but the speaker, here Donald Trump, may deny that he was telling Comey what to do. Often "hope" may aim to push toward behavior without making clear how much pressure, if any, is intended.

In summary, whatever kind of communication is involved, how it is understood is not completely separate from what listeners or readers take as the intentions of those responsible for the message. To urge that in some area, reliance should be exclusively on the text depends on special arguments we shall consider for not relying on intentions, or at least for excluding certain forms of discerning intentions.

Before turning to such concerns, I shall briefly mention questions about whose intentions matter, and what readers count for what the text conveys. In respect to a will, the intentions of the writer who has died are obviously key, since the will is designed to carry out her intentions. Things might get a bit complicated if a married or unmarried couple has reached an agreement about what the will of each would provide. In that event, one might see a will as more like a contract. How far contracts can bear on what wills do depends on state law; but, in some states, including Virginia and West Virginia, if parties had agreed on the content of their wills, the agreement can be enforced, if someone does not actually comply, by making the beneficiary under his will compensate the contract maker under equity.[2] In respect to contracts, the intentions of both parties count. A somewhat tricky question here that now applies to a high percentage of contracts is what to do when one side, such as a business, controls the terms of a contract, and a customer signs on without actual awareness of many of its specifications.

Issues about intentions become more debatable when one turns to statutes and constitutional provisions. A simple initial question is whether it ever makes sense to refer to a group intent. The answer here is obviously yes. If everyone, or the vast majority, shares an intent, the intent of the group fits with common usage. We say, "That family plans to visit New York next week," and "The faculty intends to hire someone to teach International Law." Such assertions do not entail that every single person in the group agrees with the plan or is even aware of it. In respect to pieces of legislation, at least sometimes the intention is genuinely indisputable. After the Supreme Court, in *Employment Division v. Smith*,[3] cut back sharply on the protection of the free exercise clause, Congress adopted the Religious Freedom Restoration Act.[4] Its crucial language came as close as possible to replicating that of the prior constitutional standard; the statute itself and the legislative history indicated that this was the objective, and the law was adopted with near unanimity.

Two related questions about referring to group intents are whose intents count, and count most, and whether we can have a relevant intent if the majority of those in the group have not thought about the topic. In ordinary discourse the answer to the last question is yes, and depends partly on the concept of delegation. To return to the family example, suppose all the members agree that the mother will decide where to go for the summer holiday. After the mother makes a definite decision, people would feel comfortable saying, "The family plans to be there." Within academic institutions, if a faculty committee with decisive authority decides what is to be done, it is not misleading to say, "The faculty intends to do that." In brief, at least in ordinary discourse, we have no strict standards for how many in a group must consciously intend something before we speak of a group intent. This reality, of course, does not eliminate an objection that such flexibility leads to uncertainties that should be avoided within the law. And it does not answer the question whether with complex details provided by staff members but not grasped by any actual legislators, we can plausibly refer to a legislative intent.

What I have urged so far does not tell us whose intents count most. Does "delegation" depend upon people having been assigned responsibility? With statutes, if only ten legislators actually have a view about what a provision was designed to do, should those count for much more if the ten were on the drafting committee than if they were much less involved in the actual process of enactment? And can effective delegation be given to nonlegislators?

Before addressing more specific questions about the law's treatment of intent, including whether the inquiry should be avoided because it is too difficult, I shall note a few complexities about understanding the text. What does a text mean apart from intent?

If we ask what a text itself means, and we make clear that we are not referring directly to what the writer or those voting to approve it had in mind, we are talking about what a reader would likely understand. I have urged strongly that for many communications readers will take some account of what they perceive as probable intents. This alone does not tell us how the relevant readers themselves should be conceived for ordinary discourse or for legal purposes. Two divisions are crucial here. One is how much to count those readers who are actually subject to a standard's requirement, those who may benefit from it, and more general readers who have nothing at stake. The second division involves the sophistication of readers. When we ask about which readers, a lot may well depend on what subject is involved. If one is asking about the meaning of a contract, one should probably conceive of people like those who entered into the contract. If one is referring to a "No Parking" sign, ordinary drivers should matter most. On the other hand, if a rule concerns what should be done within a particular industry, one should mainly imagine readers who are involved in that industry.

With those general observations, I shall turn to different contexts, briefly addressing what judges say about these and what seems to make sense, and trying to explain what it is about these domains that leads to different conclusions about what exactly should be taken into account.

I. WILLS

I shall start with wills, which are special in a number of ways. Wills depend essentially on the wishes of single individuals, who are largely free to decide who they want to receive their property when they die. There are formal requirements for wills, including formal witnessing by other people; these reduce the possibilities of uncertain applications and actual mistakes. Although the formal requirements of wills may typically be a bit different and somewhat greater than what people need to do in respect to various funds, such as retirement benefits, in which individuals are leaving assets to relatives and others when they die, such individuals do need to follow practices that help assure that what is written is what they seriously intend.[5]

The overwhelming emphasis on how to construe wills has depended on their texts. It is not hard to see the reasons. If the text is the product of a single person who has since died, we have a strong presumption that it reflects the intentions of the writer. The writer, of course, is not available to counter that assumption. Beyond this obvious obstacle are concerns about how the author's intent might be discerned. We could have testimony of family members, but that presents two basic problems. One is that the writer may well not have conveyed the same assumptions to different relatives, wanting each to feel he or she would receive generous benefits. Apart from the actual content of particular communications, those receiving them may have understood them in a way that is especially positive from their own point of view. We also have the possibility that those claiming benefits may lie, or be less than completely honest, about what the will's writer (the testator) told them.

All these are powerful reasons not to put great weight on subjective intentions, as contrasted with the text of the will. As we shall see, these reasons do not necessarily eliminate the relevance of intentions in some circumstances. One such circumstance is when the terms of the will do not themselves seem decisive on a particular point. Another is when a powerful basis exists to believe a mistake has been made.

If intentions are to count at all, it can matter a great deal how they are to be assessed. The difficulties I have noted are reasons to rely on external circumstances more than stated intentions, although with the tremendous increase in electronic communications that are recorded, reliance on what the writer communicated to others *may* become more acceptable than in the past when such personal interactions were often ordinary oral communications. In fact, in the electronic age, we now have many contracts that are much longer and much more detailed even if one party is unaware of many terms.[6]

It is worth noting another feature of wills. Since a person is free to change his will at any time, and also because most potential recipients do not actually see the wills of their benefactors, one cannot give great weight to likely reliance on receiving benefits. These are added reasons to prioritize what the testator meant to do, which is usually well reflected by the terms of the will.

Courts occasionally do face situations in which an outright mistake has probably been made. In one such case, a woman's lawyer had advised her to use "heirs at law" in her will, after she had asked that a residue go to her blood relations. It turned out that the family of her late husband counted as half of her "heirs."[7] In another case, the specific terms provided that at the age of forty, a daughter could receive the principal of Fund A but not Fund B; this limit was at odds with what other provisions contained, and extrinsic evidence showed that here a typist had made an error.[8] In a third case, the writer had a close friend and employee whose name was Robert W. Krause, but formally left benefits to Robert J. Krause, whom he did not even know.[9] This mistake was apparently caused by relying on a telephone book. In each of these cases, given the overwhelming evidence of an actual error in the terms of the wills, the courts allowed corrections for the carrying out of what the writers intended.

A different kind of puzzle was presented by a famous English case that has been the subject of considerable controversy. The basic question was how to construe key language that had to be understood in one of two different ways. The *Rowland* case[10] involved the will of a husband, whose assets would have gone to his brother and niece if his wife's death was "preceding or coinciding with" his own. If she survived him, she would receive his property; according to her will, her estate was to go to her niece.

The conditions under which these wills were written were that Dr. Rowland had accepted a position in which he would provide medical treatment at islands in the South Pacific Ocean. He was aware that he and his wife would be taking trips from one island to another in small ships. Two years later a small ship on which they were traveling in the Solomon Islands broke down and all on board either drowned or were eaten by fish. No clear evidence revealed exactly how and when the two Rowlands died, but if they were physically close together they probably died within seconds of each other, and even if not, the likelihood was extremely high that their deaths were not more than a few minutes apart. Given these realities, should it have been determined that their deaths "coincided"? The majority of judges in the English Chancery court concluded no. They adopted a standard of general usage in which "coinciding" was equated with "simultaneous." Given the absence of evidence that the deaths here were genuinely simultaneous, what controlled was a general law that when it was uncertain whose death preceded another's, it was presumed that the younger person outlived the older. Since Dr. Rowland was older than his wife, his assets went to her in a sense, and were actually given to her niece. Had the deaths been taken as coinciding, the husband's property would have gone to his relatives, with the niece receiving the wife's. One of the sitting judges, Lord Denning, dissented, urging that the will should be construed in light of the intentions of the writer, and "what meaning the words bore for him."

The obvious issue presented by this case is how far the language of wills should be related particularly to stated intentions or to circumstances that strongly suggest relevant intentions. We have already looked at reasons for not getting into claims about particular stated intentions, although these may not apply to intentions that are stated or discernible in written documents, and thus are not subject to uncertainties and false claims of what a person said. In the *Rowland* case, it was the circumstance that mattered. Given that these wills were written before the couple's journey to the South Pacific, and given their awareness that they would be taking risky trips on small ships, one may assume that if they had actually thought about the meaning of "coinciding," they would have assumed it covered accidents in which their lives were lost within seconds or minutes of each other. Since they definitely provided that if the deaths did coincide, the property of each would go to the relatives of each; and since if both died from the same accident at nearly the same time, the "survivor" would not be able to do anything about her "inherited" property, it would make sense to see the deaths here as coinciding. (Of course, given modern electronic devices in people's hands, it is conceivable that a person drowning now may be able to reach others in a way that was not possible more than half a century ago.)

We have a very powerful argument that if Dr. Rowland actually thought about the term "coinciding," he would definitely have assumed it covered this situation. If he had not actually considered the matter at the time of writing his will (which he did without a lawyer's help), his hypothetical intention would be that it should be seen as reaching this kind of accident. Given all this, it definitely strikes me as more sensible to interpret the will in this way.

Are there genuine counterarguments to this conclusion? One is that given the formality of wills and the need for simple applications, general terms should be given exactly the same content for all wills. This is essentially what the English court decided. That approach is too formal and unfair *if* the circumstances and highly probable intent point very strongly in a different direction. It is reasonable to adhere to a general usage *unless* the basis for a variation rests on overwhelming evidence. But if one understands general usage as strictly as did the court here, nevertheless a sufficiently powerful reason for deviating from it was met.

This brings us to an important question about general usage, one that applies to many terms we articulate. Does "coincide" always imply the same amount of a lack of gap in time? In our ordinary conversation, the answer is clearly no. A great deal depends on what we are talking about. We may say that the time two friends spent in college "coincided," if they spent the same years there. It would not matter if the initial freshman semester at one institution started one week earlier and the end of senior year was one week later. If one is giving an account of when presidents have died, one might well say that the deaths of John Adams and Thomas Jefferson, which were hours apart on the same day, "coincided." How close in time two events must be to "coincide" depends substantially on the kinds of events involved and the context in which we are drawing a time comparison. Given that for wills the crucial concern about deaths coinciding is that neither party is capable of actually using assets of the other, I believe the argument is very strong that with an ordinary will, even one made by a person not foreseeing the kinds of dangers of which the Rowlands were aware, this kind of mutual loss of life from an accident should be seen as coinciding.[11]

I am not asserting that the basic concern about ability to deal with property should completely dictate what counts as "coinciding." Suppose a couple suffers a car accident; the husband dies immediately, the wife's brain is so affected that she can no longer think or communicate, but she survives in a hospital for another month. Although the underlying reasons for her not to receive the husband's property may apply—at least if we can assume that she has plenty of resources for her medical care—the deaths did not actually "coincide." What I am suggesting is that the underlying reasons here should determine the outcome *if* the deaths can plausibly be seen as within the boundaries of "coinciding."

This conclusion relates to a more general point that is a serious issue with regard to much legal interpretation. Suppose one can conclude with some confidence that specific outcomes intended are at odds with broader purposes. People are not entirely rational about how they want to treat others, including grants of benefits. For wills, at least barring a definite change in circumstances, specific intentions should control if they are clear, even if they lie in some tension with broader purposes.

I shall mention one different conceivable reason for sticking to a narrow interpretation in *Rowland*. Suppose the Rowlands were aware of how strictly "coinciding" had been interpreted within England. Knowing that her husband had more assets, and aware of the general provision that older people are assumed to die first, Mrs. Rowland wanted to maximize the chances for her niece to be the beneficiary of the wills. She could conceivably have said that her willingness to join Dr. Rowland in the South Pacific depended on his putting in his will "coinciding" rather than "dying from the same accident." As a general point, *if* a substantial reason exists to think someone included language in a will as a concession to another's interests that did not reflect the writer's own preferences, the reason would support that application; but here the likelihood that this happened is essentially nonexistent.

II. CONTRACTS

How does the interpretation of contracts compare with the interpretation of wills? There are important similarities between these two domains, but also significant differences. Contracts, like wills, are mostly created by private citizens. Unlike wills, many contracts are not simply between individuals, but between commercial and other enterprises with each other or with individuals. Notable examples of the last are employment contracts and contracts with consumers. According to a typical contract, each party accepts an obligation to do something. Sometimes the two parties involved are roughly equal in the formation of the contract, but often one side sets the terms and the other signs on. This is what usually happens when businesses contract with employees and consumers. Whoever sets the terms of a contract, if intentions are to count, they are the intentions on both sides, though it may be argued that those on one side count more than those on the other in particular circumstances.

With at least simple contracts more than wills, a comparison with informal aspects of life may be enlightening. There are two reasons for this. The first is that people make agreements all the time with family members and acquaintances about what they will do. Two people who make such an agreement expect the other to perform, though without a legal obligation to do so. The second is that the vast majority of contractual obligations are performed without the involvement of officials. People simply do what they have agreed to do. In this respect, it may often be true such agreement occurs without much thought regarding what amounts to a legal obligation in context. An example of this is how faculty members regard obligations set by formulated university standards of their duties. Most faculty members will rarely consider which violations of those duties could lead to direct legal consequences or to a firing that would otherwise be illegal if they have tenure. Given the similarity to informal agreements and the infrequent involvement of legal officials, one important question is how far, if at all, should contracts be understood in ways that differ significantly from how we conceive agreements to engage in behavior when those agreements are not legally binding.

The answer here ties directly to what judges are capable of doing, which has implications for whether intent should count, how it should be discerned, and how the text itself should be understood, if reliance is completely on the text rather than intentions. A strong argument against considering subjective intent is that if two people are equally relevant, they may have had different intents. However infrequent that may be if all contracts are considered, when actual litigation occurs the chance of different intentions is much higher; and it is nearly certain that the parties will not then agree about intentions that are critical to the resolution of the case. This can be offered as a reason for why subjective intentions should not count at all, but a somewhat more modest and plausible approach is that they should count only insofar as they are revealed by the circumstances of the formulation of the contract, or by written documents that are not part of a contract but describe agreement about intentions, or by how the contract has been performed prior to any dispute. On this latter point, weight is typically given to what the parties have actually been doing, so long as this is not in direct contradiction to the terms of the contract itself.[12]

An interesting case that involves a number of these questions concerned an agreement made by a divorcing father in 1937 to pay his ex-wife $1,200 a year for their ten-year-old son "until" the son entered a post-high-school educational institution.[13] The father would then pay $2,200 a year for the son's time in college, up to four years. Shortly after graduating from high school, the son was drafted into the army. Should the father have continued paying $1,200? The court said no, but was that decision correct?

If we look just at the language of the agreement, we could say that the literal meaning of "until" would suggest that the father should pay up to the time that his son went to college. But suppose the son decided not to go to college, instead choosing to perform some other sort of work. Would the father then need to pay for decades to come? If the divorcing couple had seriously considered that possibility, would they not have been more explicit? Further, if the main objective of the agreement was for the father to help his former wife support the son during periods when the son was not supporting himself, would long-term financing be consistent with the basic purpose of the agreement? In 1937, being drafted right after high school did not seem likely, so the parents almost certainly did not consider that. If the divorcing couple did not actually think about that possibility, one could ask about a hypothetical intention—what would they have assumed if they had considered that circumstance? This hypothetical *might* have depended upon whether anyone in the military needed financial support and how much he would be paid. Another factor here that might count is family history. If members of both families, or at least male members, simply went to college right after high school, one might conclude that this was what the couple assumed. If, instead, it was fairly frequent for members to take low-paying jobs for a year or two before starting college, the "until" might well be taken to require payment during that period.

When we put all this together we can see how likely intentions can sometimes relate to reading understanding. On the intentions side, we can see why in this setting, specific evidence about expressed or unexpressed subjective intentions would probably be unproductive, since the father and mother would almost certainly claim different understandings. But perception of both general patterns of movement from high school to college, and the histories of the relevant families, might reveal what was either a likely actual assumption, or what would have been an assumption had the parents actually thought directly about this kind of situation.

Suppose we take only the text as counting for meaning here, with everything depending on reader understanding. What constitutes reader understanding? A reader might take "until" in a literal sense that could extend for decades. But reading the whole document, would a reader assume that money should continue going to the former wife even if the son had become completely independent and was self-supporting? A genuine reader making a serious effort would need to discern the context of the contract and take it into account.

Some of the context could be gathered by the document itself, but a reader would also consider the more specific history of these families and how they regarded the typical time connection of high school and college. How much that should count is a critical question about a textualist approach to reader understanding. If an actual reader was aware of the relevant history of those who formulated a document in a somewhat obscure way, she would take that into account in discerning what the document means. It would follow that even if one refers only to readers, one could have two documents with identical terms, but with somewhat different meanings.

Where does this lead us? Unless one takes a textualist approach as requiring strict adherence to literal terms, which is not what ordinary readers would do, it is not so simple to separate textual meaning from some reliance on likely intentions. It does bar particular forms of evidence about expressed or claimed intentions, but a review about general and more particular practices to understand the text itself is hardly distinguishable from looking at those circumstances to discern probable intentions. This amounts to simply one illustration of the reality that people generally understand what is communicated in light of what they take as the intentions of the speaker or writer.

A question that is somewhat separate from what makes intrinsic sense and from what judges are capable of doing concerns the forms of interpretation parties themselves would wish. Assuming that they do not ask for an endeavor that is too demanding, parties might actually include in a contract the way they want and expect it to be interpreted. That then becomes one aspect of both the text and their intentions. Another possibility is that certain parties, such as businesses that consistently make contracts, will generally prefer simple modes of interpretation, ones that will work against them as often as they work for them, but save them money otherwise spent on litigation. It is not irrational for these businesses to desire judicial simplicity.

What should judges do if the parties give different senses to critical terms and one is not significantly more rational than the other. One such case involved two people contracting to have cotton shipped from

Bombay to England on the ship *Peerless*.[14] In fact, there were two ships named *Peerless*, and they were going to leave at different times. Neither party knew this or initially had any idea that two ships in Bombay carried that name. When one party did not load the cotton on the first ship, the other thought he had failed to perform his duty. Given that the price of cotton had risen since the original agreement, the first party, once he understood the absence of agreement about which *Peerless*, declined to ship the cotton on the second ship. The court held that this divergent understanding meant there had not actually been a binding contract.

This makes some sense, but suppose the mistake had been trivial, that the two ships were to sail and arrive only one day apart. If either party was willing to accept the other's understanding rather than give up on the contract, would it not seem logical to conclude that the contract really did exist although the exact terms of compliance were not completely settled by it?

A somewhat similar kind of situation exists when a crucial general term is itself subject to two or more meanings, which are equally plausible. Suppose a law student from another English-speaking country undertakes to work at a U.S. law firm during the summer break. He contracts with the firm to work during the first two-and-a-half months of the summer. For him the summer starts on June 21. For this law firm and most others, let us suppose the relevant "summer" starts shortly after the end of law school examinations, sometime in mid-May. The law student here goes abroad right after his last exam. He responds to a notice from the firm by indicating his conception of summer and volunteers to show up in late June. The firm indicates that it will not accept him then. This is not a situation that will get litigated, but what should be concluded if both understandings are equally plausible? Was there no contract?

Both Restatements of Contracts have addressed such situations. The First Restatement adopted a complex objective approach for integrated contracts that what counted was "'the meaning that would be attached . . . by a reasonably intelligent person' familiar with all operative usages and knowing all the circumstances other than oral statements by the parties about what they intended the words to mean."[15] The Second

Restatement took a more subjective approach. The meaning attached by one party could prevail if he could prove what that was and that "the other party knew he did, or . . . had reason to know that he did."[16] A meaning could also prevail if that person had no reason to know the other party had a different meaning but that other party had a reason to know his meaning.

This approach seems overall to be fairer than an absolute rejection of contracts given two different meanings, but two qualifications are important. If one party actually did undeniably understand the meaning of the second party, that should control even if the second party had some reason to learn the first party's meaning but failed to do so. (One might reject this approach as being too difficult to apply, discouraging people from being honest about what they did learn.)

The second qualification concerns the strength of reasons to learn the other party's understanding. In my hypothetical situation, we can see reasons on each side. It might have occurred to our law student that what is understood as the "summer" for vacation work might not fit precisely with the calendar boundaries, and the firm might have realized that without explanation its special use of the term "summer" might not be grasped by an outsider. Here, I am not sure one party had much stronger reasons to clarify the meaning than the other, but sometimes there will be an obvious reason to check. If one party had a very strong, obvious reason to doubt that its understanding was shared, and the other party had only a weak reason to check, the second party's understanding should control. One really needs this assumption, since there may almost always be some reason to verify how a contracting party understands key terms that are not obvious.

It is worth mentioning in passing here an issue that is much more significant for statutes. What counts as a relevant intent? Suppose two people disagree about how a court should read a contract's provisions. If they were somehow discernible, should what counts be a person's hopes, expectations, or what she believes is a proper understanding? Her hopes alone should not count for much, since anyone may hope a contract will be read in a way favorable to them. If they are virtually certain how a contract will be understood by legal authorities, that may count as the parties' intentions when they formulate it *unless* they expect each other to act on different assumptions. If they are ignorant about likely legal construction, or realize it is debatable, then probably their sense of proper understanding best represents their intentions. The subtle point here is that people's relevant intentions about standards of behavior are not always how they hope the standards may be applied.

III. STATUTES

When we turn from privately created legal requirements to statutes adopted by legislatures, we quickly see some greater complications and important variables in what does and should count. In contrast to contracts and wills, citizens do not themselves decide what they will be legally required to do or how their property will be distributed. Instead a collective body of officials lays down standards to govern others. The nature of this body—in the federal United States two houses of Congress with presidential approval—the way it works, and the perceived relation between it and another branch of government, the judiciary, can bear on what may be desirable approaches for judges interpreting statutes. These factors can vary among liberal democracies, a subject explored in Chapter 4. Many of the crucial questions about statutory interpretation concern the passage of time since a statute was adopted, and issues of justice. Most of these are discussed in the next chapter.

Here the focus is on the comparative importance of text and intent when courts are called upon to apply a statutory provision fairly soon after enactment. The Supreme Court has no clear doctrine about their comparative significance although we have had some shifts over time and some more or less clear theories advanced by individual justices. For much of the twentieth century, the Court took legislative history into account as a guidance for what provisions were intended to mean. Led largely by Justice Scalia, a number of the most recent justices have emphasized textualism—that statutes should be understood in accord with what their actual terms convey.

This new development raises a number of questions, some of which we looked at in the contexts of wills and contracts. What readers count for understanding a text? What is the comparative importance of broader purposes and the specific language of provisions? What should interpreters do about obvious mistakes in the terms used? How far do perceived intentions bear on how provisions are understood? What constitutes a relevant intention? Does legislative history have intrinsic relevance for these intentions? What is needed to assert that an actual "group intent" exists? How much does it matter for many of these questions what kind of provision is involved?

Let me start with an obvious point. The fact that, in contrast with contracts, people are subjected to duties or conferred rights that they did not participate in creating bears both on the importance of reader understanding and what readers should be conceived as relevant. Here we can see a crucial difference between, on the one hand, criminal laws and other impositions of duties, as contrasted with grants of privileges and rights. For criminal laws, the argument is strong that they should be read fairly strictly and in light of what the terms themselves would say to the readers who are called upon to obey the law.

Although some crimes are limited to those working in particular domains, the typical subjects of criminal statutes are ordinary people. Since it would be unfair to punish people without a fair warning, ordinary people's understanding of the text should count a great deal unless they are informed of their duties in a way that is not closely related to the language of the statute.

How to read the grant of a privilege can be a bit different. Congress once passed a law allowing federal financing by consular officers that would provide for sailors who were stranded away from the country to be returned home. Since Alaska was part of the United States, it had no American consular officers. Nonetheless Alaskan officials provided financing for sailors, and Congress re-enacted the law without change. The

Supreme Court held that this payment was appropriate although it did not fit the actual terms of the statute.[17]

A different conferral of a kind of right, one that protected one party while limiting his opponent, was presented by *Green v. Bock Laundry Machine Co.*[18] Here the conferred right was part of the Federal Rules of Evidence, which was enacted as a statute. In legal cases, a "defendant" could preclude the testimony of a witness for the opposition if the testimony's probative value was likely to be outweighed by its prejudicial effects. Such a right made good sense for criminal defendants, given our whole system's aim to preclude unfair convictions. Civil cases are different. One expects civil plaintiffs and civil defendants to have equal rights, especially since it is often fortuitous who happens to bring a legal claim before a judge and jury. This discrepancy between criminal and civil defendants was so obvious that the Supreme Court, including the noted textualist Justice Scalia, determined that here "defendants" only meant criminal defendants, although that did not correspond with the literal text.

A different kind of interesting case concerned a law that increased jail sentencing for drug trafficking if the defendant "uses or carries a firearm." The Supreme Court majority held in *Smith v. United States* that this did apply to someone who sought to purchase cocaine in exchange for a gun.[19] Justice Scalia dissented, on the basis that "using" a firearm typically means using one as a weapon. Obviously, the term "uses" does often apply to what one employs to buy something: "I used my credit card, rather than paying cash." And the concern about fair notice for criminal liability is lessened considerably if the only concern is the length of a potential sentence, not guilt or innocence. Of course, Justice Scalia's assertion that "using a weapon" normally means employing it to do or threaten harm is correct, but we can imagine circumstances in which the shift of weapons into potentially dangerous hands is itself a deep concern. If such a concern definitely existed about drug sellers and was publicized, a reader would fairly take "uses" here in the broader sense. In brief, this case provides an example of a less than precise terminology that in any ordinary circumstances would be understood by common and expert readers in light of what they take as having been the objectives of the enacting legislature.

Even if "intentions" are intrinsically relevant to what communications mean to readers or listeners, one may believe that enactments by Congress are special. Perhaps always or often relevant intentions are missing, or are too difficult to discern to make this worth doing for judges. I shall return to these questions, but first consider what should count for reader understanding of a statute. The possible answers to that question bear on whether courts should give any distinctive attention and weight to intentions.

Let me start with a point that is obvious. Textual meaning is indisputably a crucial aspect of statutory interpretation, just as it is with wills and contracts. Legislators enact statutes that are legally binding. The texts constitute statutes in the most obvious sense, and they are the primary source for citizens and officials to discern what has been adopted. No one urges that textual meaning is irrelevant; the crucial questions are how to understand that meaning, whether it can ever be overridden, and if so on what basis. As we shall see, the distinction between overriding textual meaning and using a technique to interpret the text is not always clear. Whether a text is itself clear is not itself always a simple either-or question. Along a range of possibilities, we might speak of a provision as absolutely obvious, essentially clear, fairly definite, arguably but actually determinative, or wholly indecisive. Where in this range a provision fits can determine how it is understood and whether its apparent meaning can be overridden by other factors.

The illustration already mentioned of "defendants" being able to preclude evidence likely to be prejudicial to them provides an example of a determination that could be regarded as either a subtle understanding or an overriding. The basic idea is that it does not make sense to favor civil defendants over civil plaintiffs. I might see the Court's limitation to criminal defendants as overriding the obvious meaning of the term in the statute by curbing its coverage, but one might urge that in this context that is how the text of "defendants" should be understood. A simpler example in my own life, mentioned at the start of this chapter, involved a supposed "No Parking" violation, after I had been stopped for speeding. No driver would actually understand the "No Parking" sign to cover those who are forced to pull aside and park because of the instructions of police officers. This is a simple example of how context and clear purpose bear on what is taken as obvious textual meaning, as well as the borders of coverage if the textual term is itself arguable. Textualists are generally disinclined to play loose with specific language, but even they do not reject these sorts of considerations altogether.

Another illustration from the beginning of the chapter might be obvious in its application, but might not be so. In a large city with homeless people entering railroad stations to sleep, a passenger would not take "No sleeping in the station" as forbidding a nap while he waits for a delayed train. But the situation could be different if an aim to combat burglaries on sleeping passengers had been well publicized.

Which readers count and count most? We can ask what ordinary citizens reading an actual statute, or a sign that conveys its message, understand. We can instead conceive of those who are involved in particular fields. And we can also imagine readers who are highly sophisticated in their grasp of the force of a text. Whether the concern is overriding specific textual meaning or construing it in the best way possible, the answer here properly depends on the kind of provision involved.

If we are considering ordinary criminal statutes, and the issue is whether or not certain behavior is actually forbidden, what the statutes convey to ordinary readers is crucial. People are supposed to have fair notice that what they might do is criminal. On the other hand, suppose that a right has been granted, such as providing that the return of stranded sailors to the United States will be financed by consular officers of the federal government. Here a sailor stuck in Alaska, which lacks consular officers because it is part of the country, *might* think such an officer is really necessary for him to qualify for financial assistance or not. More important, his reading is not key. If he has really been granted a right without a consular officer needing to be involved, it does not matter if his perception would be that he has probably not qualified.

If a statute deals with a particular domain of life, such as scientific experimentation, and uses terminology that is restricted to that domain, the crucial readers should be those who are familiar with how language is used in that area. I should note here a special complication about statutes that deal with specific aspects of our social life. Often a statute will be formulated in fairly general terms—it being left to administrative agencies to provide more specific regulations. Unless the agency has actually disregarded clear provisions, its understanding may be most important, with the sense of ordinary readers counting mainly for the coverage of regulations.

How sophisticated should readers be taken to be? The *Holy Trinity Church* case provides an interesting illustration here.[20] Dispute over that case has mainly concerned the place of legislative intentions but one can see concerns that affect what a reader would understand. The law, adopted in the nineteenth century, barred American employers from making contracts with aliens living abroad "to perform labor or service of any kind in the United States." Various exceptions were specified but they did not include clergy. If one looked at the textual language in a simple way, it would include ministers, although its main coverage was manual laborers. But suppose a reader said this to herself: "Our country places a great value on the free exercise of religion. Clerics are crucial to a large number of religious practices. We have many people in this country who have immigrated from abroad and who practice religions carried out in foreign languages. Virtually all clergy for such worship are trained abroad. Whether constitutional or not, a bar on contracts with them would be a severe impairment of religious practice in the United States. For this reason, citizens and judges should read the general language as not including contracts with clerics." This conclusion makes sense whether it is seen as a construal of the language or an appropriate qualification. And, as we shall see, it is not easy to distinguish this subtle version of reader understanding from giving weight to intentions.

When we ask about reasons to deviate from what the text of a particular provision conveys, we can identify these variations: an obvious slip clearly identifiable from the text itself, a possible slip, a tension with the broader statutory purpose or accompanying provisions, an outcome that would clearly be unjust, and a conflict with intent somehow determined. How a sophisticated reader would understand a statute would depend somewhat on how it fits with what is contained in provisions in other related statutes and the broader law.

When a statute bars employers from discrimination on the basis of race, we can certainly understand that actual readers will have different views about whether this covers a favoring of African Americans in order to counter gross prior mistreatment that has, among other things, led to their receiving less valuable education, and thus being less qualified according to ordinary standards. And, of course, even recently, they have also been directly discriminated against in some employment decisions. If a reader thinks the statute should not be taken to bar various favorable compensatory treatments, we might, as with some previous examples, see this either as concluding what "discriminate" means in this context or as qualifying its actual coverage.

Even if we limit ourselves to text and reader understanding, we have identified a range of complications and multiple factors that can figure in various circumstances. The consequence is that how judges should determine reader understanding is not reducible to a simple formula that applies across the board. To say simply that judges should disregard legislative intentions does not itself actually eliminate many complexities with regard to interpreting statutes. With these observations, I shall turn to questions about intentions, many of which resemble those of reader understanding.

One issue that relates to both aspects of interpretation is whether judges should be seen as exclusively "faithful agents" of constitutionally permissible legislation, or should also function as a kind of "check" on legislators.

The prior paragraphs have made clear how far readers understand language in light of what they take those communicating to have in mind. Given the absence of an absolute distinction between reader understanding and legislative intentions, we can see that when we focus on intentions some questions about what should count are not so different from what one asks about the meaning of what has been enacted. The critical questions about intentions are: (1) how much, if at all, they should count if they are not reflected in reader understanding; and (2) what factors judges should consult to determine intentions, most notably, whether legislative history should matter.

The questions about whether intent should count independently, and, if so, how, are both controversial and somewhat complicated with statutes. The fact that for informal communications and for a statutory term such as "uses" a weapon, people generally understand what is said in light of their sense of the communicator's objectives, does not answer these questions.

One basic concern is whether there can be a relevant intent in a group of people and how often that is satisfied within a legislature. We do commonly speak about the intentions of bodies that are pursuing objectives and formulating rules. What of Congress? As noted earlier, the Religious Freedom Restoration Act followed widespread objections to the cutback of constitutional religious liberty in *Employment Division v. Smith*.[21] The objective of passing the law, clear from the text and from support of enactment, was to reintroduce the prior standard. The statute was approved by nearly a unanimous Congress. Certainly then, we can say that Congress had the intention to reintroduce prior free exercise protections.

That conclusion alone does not answer a number of questions about how often relevant intentions are actually present and the ways that judges should discern them, if they should even try. How many legislators need to have a relevant intention? Does the weight these should be afforded depend on whether legislators voted for a statute and on their particular positions? What state of mind here should count as an intention for a particular understanding? Closely related to these questions is how far "delegation" should be seen as one aspect of the legislative process. Should it be perceived as extending to staff members responsible for drafting as well as legislators themselves?

What should count as a relevant intention? As with the contract analogy, a legislator may hope for a certain judicial construal, she may think a different one is predictable based on prior judicial resolutions, and she may think something in-between is actually a proper interpretation. What state of mind should matter? If her hopes are that the judges will actually completely misconstrue the particular provision in some way, that definitely should not count as a relevant intention. What she expects judges to understand should carry some force. Her belief about proper construction should count heavily, especially if she is doubtful about how judges will conceive a provision. Not surprisingly, judges have not delved into this matter of precisely what state of mind is key. One reason is that it would simply be too hard for them to discern exactly what perspectives individual legislators had, particularly since in committee reports and speeches legislators are not likely to be candid about how far expected interpretation deviates from what they think is right, and how far each of these reflects or differs from their hopes. The second reason is that courts must rely, if at all, on the intentions of a large number of enacting legislators, who are very unlikely to have identical positions about how each of these three factors figures. Combining individual perspectives on those particular states of mind would often be essentially impossible.

What does this tell us? Conceptually when someone votes for a piece of legislation, it can be uncertain and arguable which state of mind should count as that person's intention. Of course, that does not mean intentions are always uncertain, because commonly one's hope, expectations, and sense of what is seen as right will fit together. But this does, nevertheless, reveal that "intention" in this context is not necessarily simple.

What combination of intentions of individual legislators should be needed to constitute a relevant legal intention? This is partly a question of how intent should be discerned. But the question of intention is also tied to whether judges should simply disregard particular evidence of intent and rely wholly on reader understanding. Another option would be to rest on what a "reasonable legislator would intend," without delving into actual intentions.

A critical concern about intentions involves the relevance of "delegation," but first, I shall address whether only the intentions of those who vote in favor of a piece of legislation should count. I think the "answer" is definitely no, but that turns on the complexity of the legislative process.

Typical statutes involve many provisions. Some legislators who vote favorably may not actually be content with all provisions. Do their intentions count in respect to these? Presumably yes, if one asks about their expectations and senses of proper interpretation. We can see here that even if most legislators vote for a statute, their mental states about crucial provisions may differ to some degree. If courts could discern legislators' mental states, should they say a relevant intention is absent or discern one from a combination?

A more straightforward issue is whether the perceptions that count must belong only to those who vote for a statute. Some scholars have urged yes and claimed that these should count only if they represent a majority of the legislators.[22] This view is much too restrictive. It disregards the appropriate place of delegation, and also the possible relevance of intentions of those who voted against a bill. If a statute had a single provision, it might make sense that only the intentions of those who voted in favor of it should count. But suppose a statute has multiple provisions, some of which are highly controversial, leading to an overall vote of 52 in favor and 48 opposed to the final act. On a particular provision that everyone thinks is good and favors, all those who voted no on the complete statute, and 49 who voted yes believe it has a particular content; three positive voters disagree. It would be nearly senseless to disregard the views of all those who finally voted against the bill, and to conclude that despite the views of 97 legislators, one could discern no relevant intention of the majority.

If perceived intentions matter in our lives for how language is understood, what reasons may be put forward that reliance on legislative history is, or is not, appropriate? Two important considerations here are the relevance of "delegation" and broader legislative assumptions about interpretation. I have suggested that with many groups, including families, we speak of a group intent that is in fact formulated by a segment to whom the group has assigned that responsibility. Within Congress, much of the drafting of laws is assigned to committees with work done by staff members, and their reports purport to convey their objectives. If we put aside the concern that these reports may not be consistently reliable and are influenced by interest groups, we might say that if the reports from committees in both houses of Congress are consistent *and* relevant language does not get altered subsequently, we can see those as representing congressional intent, even if most members of Congress and the committees themselves have not actually read them. As far as individual speeches before a house of Congress are concerned, those by a committee chair or by the drafter of language might be accorded significant weight as coming from those to whom this responsibility has been delegated.

Somewhat different approaches to the fact that very often most legislators will not have actual intentions about provisions or about an arguable application are to focus either on hypothetical intentions—what actual legislators would probably have intended if they had thought about the coverage of a provision, or on what a "reasonable legislator" would have intended.

Closely related to these questions about delegation is how much expertness should count for intentions. We explored this question in respect to readers; here, one might believe that if different relevant enactors have different intentions, the ones who are most expert should be given the greatest weight. Those who have drafted legislation or worked on a relevant committee might sensibly be seen as usually the most expert about content.

Given that even textualists do not deny that broader social circumstances that reflect legislators' aims can count for interpretation, what reasons may exist for urging that judges should not consider legislative history? One argument is that the history does not really reflect what most legislators actually understand. Pieces of legislative history, such as committee reports, can be seen as unreliable partly because they are not genuinely representative and partly because they are often responsive to particular special interests rather than general legislative objectives. Another basis for disregard is that it is too difficult for judges to fairly evaluate the importance of particular aspects of legislative history. Related to this is the concern that judges may often purport to rely on legislative history in order to depart from the apparent meaning of a statute when their real objective is to construe it in a way that satisfies their own values. Finally, because discerning the relevance and weight of various pieces of legislative history can be complicated, the costs of litigation may increase significantly with little reward in how statutes are construed. Even if someone acknowledges that texts are often read in accord with perceived intentions, she may urge that most actual readers of statutes will not be aware of the considerations that led to their specific language, and that it makes sense as a general legal approach to rely exclusively on the textual language itself. Although these arguments have some force, and can certainly affect how much weight to give pieces of legislative history, they are not really powerful enough to always preclude any reliance on that history.

A related question is how much the assumptions of members of Congress regarding interpretation should count for courts. Suppose a statute had a provision that said, "Insofar as the specific terms of this statute do not provide a clear answer, what is said in the committee reports of the Senate and House should carry powerful weight." Then the weight of the reports would be aspects for construing the statute, which presumably even a textualist would need to take into account. How different was the circumstance that for years courts relied on legislative history and members of Congress were fully aware of this? Whatever may be true now, one might conceive that for statutes adopted in that era, members of Congress implicitly assumed and accepted some judicial reliance on legislative history. This is one segment of the broader question of how far those who formulate legal standards should be able to indicate appropriate techniques of interpretation. Even if those who write a contract that specifies it should be construed strictly or flexibly could affect what judges would, and should, do, that does not tell us what Congress must do to have a similar influence. I do believe, however, that if most members have a basic understanding of how courts are treating statutes, that should count as a kind of implicit acceptance of that approach unless a new law or committee report indicates otherwise.

Whether one focuses exclusively on the text or gives weight to expressed intentions, the question arises how far specific language should count in relation to overall purposes. This can depend partly on the kind of statute involved. For a criminal statute, the basic provision should not be broadly extended to fulfill a purpose, given the importance of fair notice that behavior is criminal. If the issue concerns coverage that would not extend criminal liability and the basic purpose of a provision seems deeply at odds with specific language, such as the privilege of a "defendant" to bar testimony that might be prejudicial, even the textualists will not accord the specific provision its literal reading.

A much more complicated case that I explained in relation to reader understanding received substantial criticism by Justice Scalia.[23] In *Church of the Holy Trinity v. United States*, decided way back in 1892, the statute barred encouraging or assisting the migration of aliens living abroad "to perform labor or service of any kind in the United States." The overall object of the law was to preserve ordinary employment for American workers, who might suffer if aliens were brought in and hired at lower wages. The law included various exceptions including "lecturers," but did not mention ministers or priests. A historic Episcopalian church in New York City had contracted with an Anglican priest in England to become its rector. In relation to clerics, one could see free exercise values at stake in not restricting their hiring, a consideration that carried extra weight because many in this country were immigrants who went to churches in which foreign languages still dominated. Since ministers of many of those denominations, such as Russian Orthodox, were not trained in this country, reaching abroad was vitally important. If these reasons mattered, why were clerics not included in the stated exceptions that were attached to general language about "labor or service"? The answer probably is that the exceptions were included as a consequence of activity by groups that wanted to ensure they would not be restricted. One committee report did indicate that the law was not designed to reach clerics. The Supreme Court ruled that Congress did not intend to reach agreements with alien clerics. It gave emphasis to its overall purpose, and suggested that no legislator would really favor such a restriction. Justice Scalia strongly criticized this disregard of the statute's actual language.

What can we conclude? If specific statutory language is unclear, broader purposes should definitely play a role in how it is understood. If the specific language is essentially illogical in application, as with a civil "defendant," it should be qualified. If specific provisions lie only in modest tension with broader purposes, they should be applied. If the tension is much greater, a court must decide which aspect should predominate. Especially given the basic free exercise values of allowing churches to choose clerics, and the concerns about religious groups using language and practices for which virtually all clerics are trained abroad, I believe that the result in the *Holy Trinity* case was definitely right. One can see that as supported by constitutional values (a subject I shall address below), by what the intent of most members of Congress would have covered, and also by what a well-informed reader would have understood the law to reach. Also lying in the background of much of this is how far judges should see themselves as faithful agents of legislators, or as also a kind of check on unwise actions by legislators.

IV. THE CONSTITUTION

To what extent should constitutional provisions be interpreted differently from statutes and from privately created texts? There are obviously two key similarities between statutes and constitutional provisions: they have been enacted by officials and they have a general application. But we also have a number of differences that may well affect both what reader understandings and whose intentions, if any, should count. One important variation is that most parts of a constitution are directed at granting powers and imposing limits on officials that do not directly affect private citizens and enterprises. Another crucial difference is how constitutions first come into play and may be amended. In the United States and in many other countries, the amendment process is quite demanding; that renders amendment much more difficult than the enactment of a statute. These two differences have a powerful effect on how far original understanding and intentions should control, a subject explored in the next chapter; but these differences can also affect how a provision should be regarded shortly after enactment.

I shall begin discussion of this with a few clarifications. The ways in which constitutional provisions are enacted and how easy it is to amend them varies a great deal among liberal democracies, and even within the United States when one includes all state constitutions. My primary focus here is on our national constitution, which is hard to amend, requiring a two-thirds majority in each house of Congress and approval by three-quarters of the states, and which carries significant symbolic influence in the country. Before we delve into interpretation after a passage of time, how should interpreters conceive of original understanding, whether shortly after enactment or decades later? Given that a constitution is mainly focused on officials, how they are to be chosen, what duties they should perform, what powers they have (and what limits are placed on those), the perceptions of ordinary people are not central here, except when it comes to conferred individual rights, such as freedom of speech and religion. These realities might well affect how far one should conceive the actual or hypothetical readers whose perceptions matter most as persons in official positions rather than people more generally.

Of course the most important questions about constitutional interpretation concern changes over time, including basic social values. In particular, how far should judges be responsive to these changes, especially when they need to apply open-ended constitutional provisions, which are more common and central than open-ended statutes? Although addressed directly in the next chapter, these questions also bear to a significant degree on how original understanding should be conceived. If judges seek to discern that understanding, what should count and how should they discern it?

A special problem about "intentions" concerns how provisions were enacted, a complex factor for our constitution. The original document was put forward by a Philadelphia convention that was actually created to revise the Articles of Confederation, not to propose a new constitution.[24] It offered its proposal for a new constitution that was to take effect only if approved by conventions in nine of thirteen states. Leaders of the federal convention, perhaps to avoid criticism that they had exceeded their authority, indicated that what counted was the ratification, not their proposal. They did not make available records of discussions at the convention. This seemed to eliminate, or greatly reduce, the significance of those discussions. *If* what counted were the understandings within the ratifying states, which acted separately, it would be very complicated to come up with powerful evidence of governing actual intentions on any debatable questions, beyond what the text itself provided and what were discernible generally shared understandings within the broad national society. Obviously, even if one gave weight to what happened at the convention, we still have the possibility that understandings differed from those within ratifying states. For amendments to our constitution, we have proposals by Congress and ratification by states. Both have authority here conferred by the constitution, but we still have a multiple source of intentions that is less simple than the two houses of Congress that adopt statutes.

When we turn to readers, we also have complications. Insofar as readers are influenced by what they understand as the objectives of those who enact provisions, their perceptions could depend partly on which states they are in, especially if there is publicized discussion within states over whether ratification should occur.

Whether one focuses mainly on readers of the text or upon enactors, an overarching problem is that as time passes it becomes more and more difficult to discern what was the original understanding, especially since aspects of our social values may have evolved significantly over time. Are judges centuries later really able to make decisive judgments on what the range of enactors intended and the readers actually understood? Very often the answer will be no. All these complications underlie reasons here not to afford overarching significance to original understanding and intentions on debatable subjects. Insofar as these do carry weight, when judges consider open-ended provisions adopted long ago, general purposes should matter more than conceived specific applications.

As with private contracts and statutes, one important aspect of discerning meaning is recognizing what were the enactors' and readers' understandings of how interpretation occurs and should occur. Since as subjects of British supremacy we had no binding constitution, we had no history of that aspect of legal interpretation. And, of course, this was not a subject about which most readers would have developed views. Nonetheless, in the tradition of Great Britain and the colonies, interpretations of statutes and common law rules were not like that supported now by strict originalists; they were much more open to development.

An interesting problem about the relation of text and intent for open-ended provisions is whether judges appropriately reach beyond general flexible application and set more specific requirements. An interesting illustration here is *Miranda v. Arizona,* construing the privilege against compelled self-incrimination.[25] The Supreme Court held that if police failed to provide a suspect a very specific warning, his confessing or revealing of incriminating facts could not be introduced into evidence. Realistically, not every suspect the police are about to question will potentially be "compelled" to reveal information, and need a warning to avoid that. The suspect may, for example, be fully aware of his rights and believe that what he discloses will actually make him seem more innocent. But if the warning requirement broadly promotes the underlying assurance that a clause is not violated, judges may appropriately set more specific standards than the clause itself provides. This is one form of reliance on a more general purpose over what the specific language of a provision requires. Given the difficulty of constitutional amendments, this can be seen as easier to defend than with respect to contracts or with statutes, which Congress itself can alter.

These observations suggest strong similarities and differences when one compares statutory and constitutional provisions, and how these differ from privately created texts with legal force. The differences are even more striking when one considers the passage of time and changes in fundamental values, key topics in the chapter that follows.

V. ADMINISTRATIVE AND JUDICIAL INTERPRETATIONS

Although it does not, at least on the surface, directly involve constitutional interpretation, how judges respond to administrative decisions can be seen as connected to our constitutional structure. I shall start with a brief account of the place of administrative agencies, and then turn to the significant question of judicial deference.[26]

Our country has three branches of government, including courts. Legislatures, with executive approval, make laws, and the executive branches enforce them. This does not mean those with enforcement power do not make decisions on their own about what people should do. For example, those with the responsibility to see that streets are clean may be left with the power to determine which days and hours drivers will not be allowed to park on each side of the street. For the president, governors, and mayors, this enforcement power may entail some significant consequences for individuals. But the executive branch has no authority by itself to enact general laws.

Matters are a bit different for administrative agencies. Typically statutes confer on administrative agencies substantial authority to formulate regulations, and these regulations will dictate what people and enterprises must do, and what rights they have, within the domain of the agency's authority. Commonly, enforcement is also up to the agency, and often a dispute is initially considered by an agency tribunal. If the dispute eventually reaches an ordinary court, judges may be called upon to decide whether an authorizing statute grants an agency what it has assumed. They may also need to ask how a relevant statute or administrative regulation applies to the situation in front of them. A central question is whether the judges should simply make their own determination here or should defer to a greater or lesser degree to what the agency has determined.

As noted in the last paragraph, agencies typically possess powers of lawmaking, executive enforcement, and dispute resolution, as a kind of combination of three government powers. Although administrative adjudicators are not formal judges,[27] they commonly have authority, under the federal Administrative Procedure Act or some other statute, to make the initial resolution of various disputes. When these get to ordinary courts, if they do, a key question for judges is how much weight to give to what the agency adjudicators have decided. To be clear, there can be a variety of issues, and which one of these is involved can affect what should be done. The question can be about law or fact, what was actually performed, or both. A question of law might be a typical question regarding what a legal standard requires or allows, or it might be about whether Congress has conferred on an agency discretion about how to treat a subject. On the content of legal standards, we have both statutes and administrative regulations; does it matter which is under review?

Before delving into these, I should mention that we have significant differences in the nature of agencies. Many of these are essentially parts of the executive branch, whereas others are "independent" agencies, such as the Securities and Exchange Commission and the Federal Trade Commission. On these bodies, commissioners are appointed for fixed terms and can only be dismissed with formal cause. Just how far the president has control over what various agencies can and must do is itself a controversial question, which is gathering significant importance under Donald Trump's presidency and the actions he has chosen to take.[28]

The Administrative Procedure Act, adopted in 1946, is a key statute for what administrative agencies may do and how decisive their decisions should be.[29] The statute was based largely on a political and legal history during the Depression and World War II that encouraged agencies to do what would help the country.[30] A substantial part of the statute's language is fairly open-ended, and its directed interpretation has shifted over time with changing Supreme Court doctrines, becoming more textualist in recent decades. Among other things, the statute provides reviewability when an agency has reached final determinations, even if no one has yet suffered negative consequences.

A simple and important distinction with regard to judicial review is between facts and legal requirements. For a court reviewing the decision of an initial tribunal, deference about determinations of fact is bound to be greater than determinations about what the law requires. When one thinks of ordinary legal cases, appellate courts afford no deference to district court judges about the content of the law, but whether factual determinations are by juries or district court judges, appellate judges will accept them unless they are wholly implausible. The legal determinations also receive more review for agency determinations, but appellate judges afford more deference for these than they do for interpretations of district courts. When it comes to facts, they exercise somewhat more judgment on their own than they do reviewing ordinary legal cases.

Determinations of law can be deferential in two different ways. The simplest is a decision that Congress has simply conferred on the agency a discretion to decide who or what will count for a particular purpose. The Administrative Procedure Act precludes review of a determination "committed to agency discretion by law" although it also has a provision that allows review of "abuse of discretion."[31] An example of when this discretion came into play was a 1944 decision that the National Labor Relations Board could determine that someone who sold newspapers on the street counted as an "employee" of a newspaper publisher since "[t]hat task has been assigned primarily to the agency. . . . "[32]

A second difference is between the legal content of statutes and of agency regulations. Not surprisingly the degree of deference has been greater when an agency interprets its own regulations. Here any "plausible" interpretation of regulatory language will be accepted.[33]

What is both notable and controversial is the standard of judicial review of administrative determinations of law that extend beyond the scope of their own regulations. In the crucial case of *Chevron U.S.A. Inc. v. Natural Resources Defense Council*,[34] decided in 1984, the Supreme Court established a standard of substantial deference, including this language: "[I]f the statute is silent or ambiguous with respect to the specific issue, the question for the court is whether the agency's answer is based on a permissible construction of the statute." This has been taken as a high degree of deference, implying that very often an agency interpretation will survive whether it is made one way or the other.

We can identify arguments for and against this high degree of deference. The simplest argument in favor is that agencies are in a superior position for understanding the implications of statutes that apply to them, and that courts should go along unless the positions are actually unreasonable.

A second reason for deference includes the scope of jurisdictions. Relatively few cases get to the Supreme Court. If a district court or court of appeals is involved, and it decides in a certain way, that will control only the territory within its jurisdiction. Given the national coverage of a typical federal agency, it may well decide to stick with its position in the rest of the country. Obviously, if an agency is treating governing standards differently in different regions, that will seriously complicate how it operates and likely be confusing and economically inefficient. This is one strong argument why federal courts generally should afford deference to administrative determinations.

The contrary argument is that the business of courts is to decide what laws require: in other kinds of cases, federal courts do not defer to local officials or to state tribunals, and giving a special status to administrative agencies is unwarranted. Put more strongly, it can be urged that the degree of deference is actually unconstitutional, failing to satisfy the division of powers that confers on courts the authority to decide questions of law.[35] Given that courts do not defer to legislative interpretations of statutes, they should not be deferring to administrative interpretations, according to an argument that rejects *Chevron*.

The degree of deference indicated by *Chevron* has been controversial. This depends partly on political realities, whether one is more sympathetic with the outlooks of most presently sitting appointed judges or the dominant agencies. I will not explore this problem, but like most standards of interpretation, the actual application of the *Chevron* approach has shifted over time, being qualified and limited in various ways in more recent cases.[36] What is crucial for our purpose is perceiving that a very important aspect of understanding statutory and regulatory language is how far courts will try hard to decide a legal issue as accurately as possible, and how far they will defer to determinations made by others.

VI. JUDICIAL DEFERENCE: IS IT CONSTITUTIONAL?

So far we have looked mainly at text and intent, and specific provisions versus overall purposes, on the general assumption that the role of judges is to determine the best answer. However, as the last section shows, in a significant number of cases, things are a bit different. Judges may accept what officials in the executive branch or independent agencies have done, including interpreting statutes and their own regulations, unless that is clearly unconstitutional or unreasonable. When that happens, the effective "law" can be different from what judges would have determined if they had tried their best to reach an independent determination. Although this practice takes somewhat different forms, it amounts to deference. Neither the underlying bases nor the question of how far this is warranted is simple. This section briefly explores this further.

The deference approach involves both questions of statutory and constitutional interpretation. Sometimes a case may involve only the appropriate interpretation and application of a statute, but often the question is whether in general or a specific application of a statute or regulation amounts to a constitutional violation. For example, the Fifth Amendment to the original Constitution allows the government to take property for "public use" if it provides just compensation. As with most specified rights in the Bill of Rights, it is now assumed that this applies to the states. Suppose a state transfers property from one private individual or enterprise to another, claiming that this will serve public welfare. Does this count as "public use"? If not, the Constitution is being violated.

A rather different, more general, constitutional question is the role of the judiciary in the separation of powers. If one thinks that the judiciary was created to act independently, one may believe that many or most forms of deference to other officials are really unwarranted, especially if some constitutional question is at stake. Even if no independent constitutional issue is involved, one could still see deference as a failure by judges to perform their constitutional duty. One way of phrasing this would be to see the practice as a violation of the "rule of law" that is an aspect of our constitutional democracy.

When a court reviews what an agency has determined, it may purport to employ one of three standards of review: strict scrutiny, rational basis, or an intermediate approach. If the government is clearly restricting freedom of expression, strict scrutiny will be involved. The constraint will be upheld only if it is needed to serve a compelling interest. For most economic regulations, only a "rational basis" needs to be met. Some have objected to this approach as actually unconstitutional. Before addressing this question, I shall briefly sketch a bit of the underlying history.

Prior to the mid-twentieth century, claims of violation of property and economic rights received substantial review of the kind represented by the controversial *Lochner* case, in which the Supreme Court held that a law limiting the working hours of bakery employees constituted a violation of due process.[37] Over time, and especially with the New Deal, the review of such laws became more and more relaxed.[38] In *United States v. Carolene Products Co.*, the Supreme Court upheld under a relaxed rational basis test a law barring the fortification of dairy products with vegetable oil.[39] In 1955 in *Williamson v. Lee Optical*, the Court accepted a law that limited which opticians could fit eyeglasses, although the apparent aim was to protect those licensees from competition.[40] It was enough that the law "might" have been motivated by health and safety concerns. In a later decision the Court treated a choice as acceptable if "any reasonably conceivable state of facts" could provide a rational basis.[41] In more recent years, the courts have not always applied the rational basis tests in this relaxed form. In various circumstances, they have explored actual legislative aims and the appropriateness of application; this has been characterized as rational basis "with bite," and one might see it as amounting to a kind of intermediate scrutiny. Rather than delving into these nuances, I will briefly explore the more basic constitutional questions.

Some have urged that the Constitution does protect individual economic rights, so that these should not be seen as radically different from subjects such as free speech.[42] In addition to basic protections against any imposition, one may have a right to be treated fairly in relation to others. This is one way to see the case that some opticians were being disfavored in relation to others.

Apart from an extension of persuasive equal protection arguments, the typical proposal is that the "due process" requirement demands much higher judicial scrutiny. The basic idea has to be that if legislators or executive officers act inappropriately in relation to individuals, they have violated due process. Although this particular claim gets some support from the Supreme Court's use of the "due process clause" of the Fourteenth Amendment to apply many original constitutional protections to the states, it is really an extreme stretch of the constitutional text.

The original Constitution and the Bill of Rights contain numerous conferrals of power and protected rights. Amendment V deals mostly with limits on criminal process. After a semicolon, it says "nor shall be compelled in any criminal case to be a witness against himself, not be deprived of life, liberty, or property, without due process of law. . . ."[43] If the original Constitution actually protects economic rights generally, it is very hard to say this is done by the text of the due process clause. Section I of the Fourteenth Amendment provides that "No State shall make or enforce any law which shall abridge the privilege or immunities of citizens of the United States; nor shall any State deprive any person of life, liberty, or property, without due process of law . . . ."[44] Especially given the earlier Fifth Amendment, it is much more plausible to see legislatures or administrative agencies treating people unfairly as a denial of "privileges and immunities" than of "due process."[45] In the late nineteenth century, the Supreme Court interpreted "privileges and immunities" very narrowly and, as a consequence, the coverage of the due process clause has been extended well beyond what a natural textual understanding would support.

This leaves us with the more fundamental questions: What should be seen as constitutional rights, and how rigorous should court review be? Whatever may have been the original sense of how an economy operates, we now see extensive government involvement as appropriate. Especially given the limited geographical coverage of federal courts other than the Supreme Court, it makes sense to afford some deference to what the federal government is doing nationally. Some reasons also support similar deference to individual states. On the other hand, judges should seek to protect against what is obviously unfair, and that should include some assessment of why legislators or executive officers probably acted as they did, not accepting everything that could "conceivably" have been based on legitimate grounds. What makes sense would be a somewhat more rigorous version of a rational basis test than its most relaxed version. We all need to recognize that just how rigorous the test should be will depend partly on what is being regulated, what groups are affected, and how the application works. But this remains a domain in which ordinary review should be less strict than if free speech or cruel and unusual punishment is involved.

VII. CONCLUSION

This chapter has explored a wide range of issues concerning how far text and intentions should figure in judicial interpretation of legal standards and what should constitute the relevant understanding of a text and the intentions of those who enact it. We have also looked at the practice of judicial deference to the interpretations of others and whether that is appropriate.

The chapter makes two fundamental points. The first is that intrinsically what a communications means is closely interrelated to the perceived intentions of those who make it. Any plausible argument for disregard of intentions must rest on claimed specific obstacles, not ordinary understandings. The second basic point is that how to understand text and intentions is sometimes simple, but when it comes to debatable situations each can be complicated and controversial. We should not suppose that focus on each or both will easily resolve difficult cases that reach the Supreme Court.

2

Changing Conditions and Conflicts with Values

This chapter focuses on two kinds of situations that go beyond discerning original meaning. One is when significant circumstances have changed since a legal standard was formulated; the other concerns certain basic conflicts or tensions between articulated standards and basic values, such as fairness between contracting parties and, more generally, fundamental concepts of justice and social welfare. A reader rightly sees these as two different kinds of questions about how to apply legal standards, but covering them together makes sense because often they are closely linked.

Although changes in ordinary conditions can make the application of a standard much less fair than it was when originally formulated, much more troublesome for some statutes and many constitutional provisions are basic changes in social values. These can be perceived in terms of general cultural norms or what judges understand as a correct evaluation. To take a simple illustration to which we shall return, at the time of the Bill of Rights, capital punishment was an authorized penalty for all sorts of crimes, including theft and homosexual behavior. It is now viewed as constitutionally foreclosed except for crimes that include the taking of lives of others and for especially threatening offenses such as treason. Before I turn to statutes and constitutional norms, I will begin with wills, contracts, and trusts that lead to cy-pres.

I. WILLS

Since a person can revise her will up to the time she dies, and the terms of a will are carried out shortly thereafter, the chances of changed conditions are not extensive. And given that people can do almost anything they want with their wills, the concerns about fairness and social justice are minimal. On the latter point, it is important that many state laws require that people do leave some assets to spouses when they die.[1] Also in play is a policy that favors including unspecified new children, unless the will indicates to the contrary.[2]

Three actual changes in circumstances do present questions of how a court should respond. Suppose the writer of the will believes her son has died, for example, in military conflict. She omits him from her will. However, shortly after her death, it is learned that the son is still alive, having been kept for months in a prisoner's camp by our country's enemy. Barring clear evidence that the will writer actually disfavored this child, it makes sense to construe the will as granting him an amount equal to that of the other children. The theory would be that this outcome is plainly what she would have written had she been aware of the actual facts.

The second situation is a bit more complicated. Suppose a couple gets divorced after the husband has written his will. Should the former wife still receive what the will provides for her? Two arguments support yes being the answer. The first is that the husband could have changed his will; his not doing so indicates that he was content with what it provided. A second, somewhat related, point is that in this day and age the circumstances for divorce vary radically. For many, hostility and resentment do figure as major factors. For others, the main feeling is a sense that it is time to lead separate lives. This can fit with continuing respect and affection for the former spouse, which can be true even if one or both partners have a new romantic involvement. When these positive views continue, a husband may not mind his former wife receiving a good bit of his property.

What competing reasons lie against merely enforcing the will's terms? The truth of the matter is that for most of us, what our will provides is hardly our dominant concern in life. Given the connection of our wills to our deaths, we have a kind of inclination to focus on other subjects. Thus, it is easy to conceive of someone who has been divorced, who would not want his property to go to his former spouse, but who has not taken the effort to reformulate his will. This likelihood, of course, decreases as time passes. It is much more probable for someone who was suffering from an illness at the time of divorce and died a month later than for a healthy man who did not die until fifteen years after the divorce. The suggestion that a judge asked to enforce a will should take these factors into account makes intrinsic sense. Regrettably, it does not yield a clear and simple application of when specific terms should be disregarded.

The third kind of changed circumstance raises a much more substantial public policy concern. Suppose that a person who would recover under the will actually killed the testator? Under existing law, such a person may not receive what was specified. In the famous case of *Riggs v. Palmer,* decided in 1889,[3] New York's highest court determined that a grandson who killed his grandfather could not receive under his grandfather's will, although the governing statute provided no such specific bar. The court, essentially relying on the basic common law principle that people are not allowed to profit from their own criminal acts, construed the statute dealing with wills to include that limit. One might, of course, assume that most people who write wills would not want those who kill them to recover, but that was not the court's basis for decision.

An interesting question is raised by a clear contrary intent. Suppose the grandfather had been aware that his grandson had a mental illness problem, and an inclination to violence, including moments of anger against the grandfather. Suppose he decided that he wanted to help finance recovery for the grandson no matter what. And he thus provided in the will itself, "Even if he happens to kill me, I still want him to receive under this will." Should public reasons to discourage killing control even against such clear intentions? This is a hard question, but my guess is that most courts would still bar recovery, at least if the killing was definitely intentional and did not fall into the category of assisted suicide.

II. CONTRACTS

How should contracts be understood if they conflict with basic values or conditions change? If contracts actually require behavior that is illegal or directly contrary to basic legal values, they will be unenforceable. A central way that conditions might, in a sense, change is if the parties are themselves carrying out the contract in a way that does not actually fit its terms. This could be a basis for a conclusion that the contract should not be interpreted according to the text and its terms, or for simply treating the settled performance as establishing the obligations that matter. A more obvious basis for not enforcing a contract's terms is if carrying them out has become impossible or the planned benefit for one side has disappeared.

A simple example of this is when the ability to render one's contractual obligations has become effectively impossible. If an owner rents a dance hall for a company to use a month after the contract is formed, and the hall burns down three weeks later, the company's planned performance has become impossible.[4] The owner cannot supply the hall and does not need to pay damages for whatever loss the renter may suffer from not being able to provide the performance. A slightly different situation is when a party's stated obligations become incredibly expensive and performing them would yield no or minimal benefits. In classic cases, people had agreed to rent rooms for a day or slightly longer in order to witness a British king's coronation parade. The parade was cancelled because the king was ill. The courts held that the potential renters did not have to pay what they "owed," but they could not recover money they had already shifted to the owners of the rooms.[5] Although it is arguable whether they should have been allowed to recover that amount, especially since the rooms could be rented again for a later date on which the coronation parade would actually be held, the renters not having to pay the full amount was obviously fair. According to the Restatement, when the purpose of a contract is frustrated, remaining duties to render performance are discharged.[6]

A more interesting and difficult situation is when the actual terms of the contract can be carried out and both parties can receive the specified benefits, but that consequence would be unfair to one of the parties, and, according to an overwhelming probability, at odds with an underlying assumption when the contract was formed. In *Steuart v. McChesney,*[7] the Pennsylvania Supreme Court considered such a case. A couple had agreed with their neighbors that if they chose to sell their property, and had received a bona fide offer, the neighbors could purchase the property according to the value set by the tax "assessment rolls." After her husband died, the widow decided to sell the property. She had actual offers of $30,000 and $35,000. The neighbors offered her $7,810, twice the assessed value of the tax rolls, which were purported to be at one-half of market value. In fact, the tax rolls had not been reformed for a number of years and their set value was far below half of actual market value. The court enforced the specific terms of the contract, relying heavily on the parol evidence rule, which barred evidence concerning the plain terms of a contract.

Was this fair? The trial court had indicated that the terms of the contract were designed to provide mutual protection, but this was not really accurate. The neighbors had no duty to buy the property in any circumstance; they were merely afforded a right to buy it under certain conditions if they wished. The duty fell on Mrs. Steuart to sell to the neighbors at a certain price rather than to someone else. Barring any indication that the neighbors had paid the Steuarts something substantial for this contract, its terms clearly amounted to a kind of friendly concession to a neighbor rather than any exchange of significant benefits. On this understanding, to require a sale for way less than the actual market price was grossly unfair.

Two arguments were available that the parol evidence rule should not have barred underlying evidence. One is that such evidence should be available to indicate an overall purpose, if not the meaning of specific provisions. The other is that we could understand the contract as based on an implicit assumption that the agency responsible for tax rolls would actually set an amount that would approximate half of the real market value. This was clearly a likely assumption, however well it fit with actual agency practice. Since the neighbor had no obligation to buy if the value was too high, and thus the Steuarts were not gambling in favor of this, it makes sense to conclude that the parties were assuming the standard would be set fairly in terms of the genuine value of the property. On that understanding, a condition set by the contract had not been met.

Applying the specific terms in the case produced an intrinsically unfair result that was almost certainly at odds with the broader original purpose and with what the parties assumed would take place. Given all the realities, it would have been much better to allow more evidence about original understanding, or simply to rule that the overall content of the contract indicated that under the actual purpose, the price must come much closer to a fair sense of market value.

III. CY-PRES

Although contracts are usually enforced according to their actual terms, we have seen that sometimes radically changed conditions or conflicts with the basic purpose of the contract can lead to different results. The judicial power and justification for altering the effects of specific terms has been much clearer with trusts that are set up to last over time. As time goes by and conditions change, trustees and judges may end the trust and have resources revert to heirs or in effect alter terms set by the grantor who has died some time ago. The basic idea for the latter approach is that if applying the original terms becomes impossible, impractical, or illegal, actual application shall be shifted to a practice that still promotes the major purpose while loosening "the dead hand of the past" over modern expenditures of charitable resources. I will refer to a few illustrations of this practice, and to some of the uncertainties it creates about what should be done. Two central questions are: How far should actual donor intent or desirable uses of resources control, and what evidence should count for intent?

To take a hypothetical illustration in respect to intent, suppose three donors each provide resources to go over time to a local medical facility. If, as time passes, the existence of that facility proves no longer necessary, should the money go to a medical facility at another location, to a nonmedical local charity, or revert to family members? Suppose the first donor has supported the facility only because a relative is running it. She might prefer a reversion to family members. The second donor has wanted crucially to advance medical availability. The third donor cared essentially about improving life within his community. These differing perspectives could determine which option would help fit each donor's intent. Exactly what evidence, if any, should a court consider for this that is not contained in the grant itself? Judges might ask a more general question about what a "rational donor" would want here, but that would not provide any clear answer to this problem. Courts may at least take the approach that donors have a dominant aim of promoting a charitable purpose unless clear evidence indicates the contrary.

In what became an actual case in 1978, a man who had helped found a Unitarian Church provided a trust to support it.[8] His will provided that if the church "change[s] its religious tenets and cease[s] to inculcate a Liberal Religion,"[9] a gift over would go "to support Unitarian education at Harvard and the poor of Mclean Asylum." The church did not become illiberal by endorsing more traditional Christian doctrines, but it did dissolve. The Unitarian-Universalist Association sought to receive the gift, and judges had to decide if that should happen or if the specific terms of the will for the consequence of doctrinal change should be followed. Here it would be very hard to determine a relative donor intent with confidence. My own guess would be that the donor might well have approved a shift to the larger Unitarian organization if its doctrines had not changed, but given the donor's failure to mention that possibility, probably the court's disposition to carry out the specified shift was appropriate.

A different kind of case involved the America's Cup yacht races. The latest deed of 1887 had various terms for the races but also allowed potential challengers who wanted to enter the race some year to alter various conditions that the 1887 deed had set. By 1988, general practices were established and well-settled; these provided equal opportunities for countries that wanted to participate. In that year, however, a New Zealand club made a single nation challenge to the San Diego Yacht Club, which held the cup. It proposed a size of ship far out of then-established practice, and its single-country challenge was strongly at odds with what had become well-accepted. The court refused to apply cy pres and left the New Zealand challenge, which fit the terms of the 1887 deed, in force.[10]

For two reasons, this decision seems misguided. The most obvious is that if one focused on what those who formulated the terms would want, it is highly likely that they would want to have practices that were working fairly in general application to be carried forward. The second reason concerns their degree of support of the America's Cup itself, as that related to all that was involved in the practices as they existed in 1988. The "cup" for which they were responsible was a miniscule part of the total expenses undertaken by countries participating in the competition. In these circumstances, it makes much more sense to give overriding emphasis to what works well. Although some complications in the case suggest that the final problem could have been avoided, here it would have been more sensible to require a deviation from specific terms if adherence to them interfered with fundamental fairness for all countries seeking to engage in a competition each time one took place.

My final illustration presents problems that are particularly complex and difficult. In the nineteenth century after slavery was abolished but while racial segregation in the South was still common, Senator Augustus Octavius Bacon provided money for support of a public park for white women and children. The Supreme Court ruled in 1965 that public parks could not be segregated by race. This ruling left it up to Georgia courts to determine if the state should use the funds to support integrated parks or to return the gift to Senator Bacon's heirs. Those judges ruled that the money should go to the heirs, and that was upheld by the United States Supreme Court.[11]

That case raises both the questions of how much the intent of the donator should count and how it should be conceived. If a lengthy time has passed since the original grant, one might think that donor's intent should fade in importance as compared with what now seems valuable. A more complex question here is how a person's intent should be taken. Let us suppose that Senator Bacon definitely accepted and approved of racial segregation but did not want to reintroduce slavery or radically constrain opportunities for black people. We might characterize him as a kind of moderate on how racial issues were then perceived. If we could so identify him, should his specific perceptions control completely in the present, or should one assume a kind of shift over time?

Let me explain what I mean with a personal illustration. When I was in college and in subsequent years, I considered myself a liberal on major social issues, an outlook that fit with what my parents had taught me. After my junior year of college, I lived for a summer in the very poor neighborhood of East Harlem; without pay, I provided forms of help to young members of minority groups. In the summer before I started teaching, that is 1965, again without pay, I worked for a month in Jackson, Mississippi, for the Lawyers' Committee for Civil Rights. In these ways, I made efforts to fulfill what from a liberal point of view I regarded as just. At that stage of my life, like many others with generally liberal inclinations, I did not approve punishment for homosexual behavior but did not see same-sex marriage as something that should be definitely authorized legally, much less established as a constitutional right. As times have changed, so have my outlooks. Same-sex marriage now seems to me to be obviously just and desirable. What my personal example is meant to illustrate is that to a large extent people with certain inclinations are highly likely to develop different views over time about specific subjects as a culture and perceptions of values develop. If Senator Bacon was actually a moderate and had simply lived until 1965, he might well have come to accept interracial parks as fully appropriate. Certainly that has become true of the vast majority of people in the South.

I am not suggesting that if Senator Bacon had specifically provided that if the segregated park could no longer exist, his relevant money should go to his heirs, that provision should have been disregarded. But in the absence of such specific language, I think it would be sound to view donor's intent not exclusively in terms of perceptions at the time of the donation, but largely in terms of what a somewhat similar individual would be likely to believe given the passage of time. Of course, I acknowledge that this is not a simple standard to apply, but often it is also very difficult to discern the specific intentions of those who lived many decades ago.

Closely resembling cy-pres for trusts is a doctrine that when restrictions or servitudes for real property are no longer accomplishable because of changed conditions, judges may terminate or modify them. An interesting case, *El Di Inc. v. Town of Bethany Beach*,[12] involved what covenants landowners had to agree to when they bought property, namely that no one would sell alcohol on his premise. Absent unanimous agreement among the existing landowners, getting rid of such restrictions is usually impossible. By the time the court decided this case, Bethany Beach had become a popular resort, alcohol could be purchased nearby, and people attending restaurants were allowed to drink alcohol they had brought with them. The court's majority concluded that all this made the intended benefits of the covenant unattainable, and it allowed the restaurant, which offered the doubtful claim it could better control drinking if it sold alcohol than if it let people drink their own, to disregard the restriction. As with the cy-pres doctrine, the court ruled that the justifications for the changed condition approach rested both on implied intent and public policy.

Not acknowledged by the court, this case raises a really fascinating question about whose intent should count for restrictive covenants. The originally quiet town of Bethany Beach was formed largely by the Christian Missionary Society of Washington D.C., a group that believes people should not drink alcoholic beverages. Most of the original purchasers of property here undoubtedly held this view and welcomed a "dry" environment. The percentage of the later purchasers who shared this outlook almost certainly declined, although they understood the actual restriction if they paid any attention to it. If we ask about the original purchasers who believed on religious grounds that alcohol should not be sold for drinking, they would probably have wanted the restriction to continue even if its actual effectiveness had diminished greatly. But later purchasers might well have seen the restriction as pointless, and possibly reducing the value of their property to a modest degree. In this context, whether acknowledged or not, it makes sense for the original intent to fade in force if its aspirations are not shared by most modern owners of the property, even if they do understand what the restriction limits. That is partly because these covenants are not like contracts that people can negotiate. If a restrictive covenant covers a range of properties, you must accept it if you want to buy one of those properties. The argument for giving less force to what the original creators perceived is supported not only by the fact that later purchasers must sign on the restrictive covenants, but also the fact that the value of restricting the sale of alcohol had much diminished given all else that had occurred that made alcohol easily available.

IV. STATUTES

As with text and intent, matters become more complicated in certain ways when we turn to statutes and constitutions. As we shall see, in the United States the most crucial questions about changes over time concern our Constitution. Looking at these changes exposes many of the deep flaws of an originalist approach that focuses overwhelmingly on originally perceived applications. Before turning to those concerns, I shall begin with statutes.

When one asks about conflicts with values, our federal and state statutes are clearly related to the national Constitution and state constitutions. Simply put, the crucial values coming from beyond a statute are those of the constitutions. If a statutory provision is at odds with a relevant constitution, it is invalid. There are two, somewhat related, qualifications here. One is judicial deference. On various subjects, as described briefly in Chapter 1, judges will defer to the judgments of those in the other branches of government. What this entails is that if the coverage of a law or a specific application could reasonably be seen as constitutional or unconstitutional, a court may accept its validity even though absent deference it might have reached a contrary conclusion. A more extreme drawing back is the "political question" doctrine. If the specific issue concerns relations between branches of government, notably the powers of the president and Congress, the U.S. Supreme Court has sometimes declared that it will not involve itself in that issue.

Constitutional values can figure in construing a statute, as well as whether it should be declared invalid. Here we have both one simple, obviously sound, approach and two aspects of what the Supreme Court has done that are more debatable. First, suppose that there are two competing ways of understanding statutory language or its application that are equally plausible; one of these would definitely be unconstitutional, the other would not. A judge will interpret the statute in a manner that she regards as constitutional in this situation.

Things are a bit different if the understanding that is unconstitutional has the greater force. Should judges simply use ordinary techniques to determine meaning and application and then consider constitutional validity, or should they stretch what the statute entails so that it avoids being invalidated? Judges do not explicitly acknowledge that they are taking the latter approach, but in certain cases they do adopt an understanding that would be unconvincing if one did not consider constitutional limits. Of course, one might defend this approach as actually serving the purposes of legislation. Would not legislators broadly want their statutes to be maintained, even if qualified in ways they did not actually choose, rather than having what they did struck down?

Another technique that relates to the one just discussed is more arguable. In some cases, the Supreme Court will prefer an interpretation that is in less tension with constitutional values, even though it is not clear that it would actually hold the most evident understanding to be invalid. This may, of course, be simply a failure of disclosure in an opinion, but sometimes it may mean that the judges have not resolved the constitutional question, or even that they do not believe that a clear definite legislative directive of that sort would actually be unconstitutional. It is genuinely debatable whether a court should interpret a statute in a way that is definitely less plausible if the more plausible reading lies in tension with constitutional values although perhaps is not actually unconstitutional. On the one hand, one can say that this is judges interfering with a legislative choice; on the other, one might see this as a function judges use to help legislators move in desirable directions.

One example of this kind of situation involved the Draft Act, which had been amended to make clear that in order to succeed a pacifist seeking exemption had to have a standard religious objection to military service, including a typical belief in God. The Supreme Court interpreted that to cover objectors who did not have such beliefs. In *Welsh v. United States*,[13] four justices took this position. Justice Harlan concluded that the act's favoring religious objectors over others was an unconstitutional violation of the establishment clause, and so he voted with the four justices for the broader coverage.[14] These four effectively read the statute itself in a highly strained way without indicating whether the more obvious reading would draw a line that was unconstitutional.

When we put aside concerns about unconstitutionality, do we have reasons to see the content of statutes effectively revise over time? Consider the Mann Act adopted more than a century ago. It prohibits transporting women across state lines for "prostitution or debauchery, or for any immoral purpose." Clearly, not every immoral purpose ever qualified. If a New York resident took his wife to a football game in New Jersey because he wanted her to suffer over the loss of her favorite team, one could see that as "immoral," but not covered by the statute. But in a 1917 case, *Caminetti v. United States*,[15] the Supreme Court ruled that the act did reach a man's transporting his mistress to another state under a plan to engage with her in sexual intercourse. With sharp increases in divorces and the acceptance of sexual relations outside of marriage, the defendant's purpose would not now seem "immoral" by community standards, at least if he was not married to someone else. In this instance, one could say that the basic meaning of "other immoral purpose" has not really changed, but that its applications have.

The question of the passage of time has been significant in relation to laws that provide equal rights for black citizens or prohibit "discrimination." In 1866 following the Civil War, the Civil Rights Act guaranteed black citizens equal rights to contract. Although determining original intentions and understandings becomes more difficult as time passes, the aim was to provide blacks a basic equal legal status. In 1968, in *Jones v. Alfred H. Mayer Co.*,[16] the Supreme Court ruled that the law forbade private parties from discriminating against blacks in the sale of property. If this was a kind of extension, it was one that conformed to developing social values.

Examples such as this suggest that as time passes, broader purposes should have increasing significance in relation to specific applications, at least if the broader purposes are still seen as desirable and the statute is cast in fairly general language. Relatedly, one can regard modern reader understanding as directly related to how a statute should be conceived. That can shift with the passage of time and developing social values. One clear example of when modern reader understanding should count concerns a provision that criminalizes behavior. Suppose that decades ago people would understand that the language reaches particular actions that modern readers would not regard as being covered. Given the crucial general principle that people should receive "fair warning" of what behavior is criminal, judges would have powerful reasons not to read the provision at this time to cover that behavior.

Connected to all this is the idea that although legislatures can clearly revise laws and adopt ones that are in serious tension with others, when courts construe and apply statutes, they should do so in a way that fits well with other statutes and the common law, unless they have strong bases not to do so. Of course, a pure originalist might say everything in that respect should depend on the scope of the law at the time of enactment, but that has not been the approach in this country. If the surrounding law at the time of judicial decision has changed in basic features since enactment, this can support a developing understanding of what a statute itself does.

Two points are worth noting here. If someone asks, "what did the enactors conceive about interpretation over time, or what would they have conceived if they had thought about it?," he might conclude that they would have wanted adjustment to changing conditions and values. This approach gives weight to actual perceived intentions about interpretation or to one aspect of hypothetical intentions—what actual enactors or reasonable ones would have concluded if they had thought about it.

The second point concerns the importance of organizations of liberal democratic governments for how courts should deal with these questions. In Great Britain, the queen has signed any adopted law, and the political parties have been constituted so that the dominant party has the prime minister, and party members will vote for laws backed by their leadership. Statutory language has tended to be more clear and coherent than with many United States compromises, and it has not been as difficult to obtain new enactments. It is often hard in our country. Given these differences, one may conclude that sticking with original understanding and intentions is a much sounder approach in Great Britain, since needed corrections will typically not be too difficult to obtain legislatively. By contrast, the complexities of getting laws adopted and revised in the United States can be seen as reasons for the courts to take a more active role in bringing older statutes and their applications up to date in light of modern law and modern values.

I shall briefly mention complexities introduced by the place of independent agencies in the making and application of law. In many areas, fairly general statutes confer on agencies the authority to make appropriate regulations. The most direct standards to which affected parties pay attention will be those set by the agency regulations. How far should judges accept agency understanding of statutes and their specific regulations? In brief, courts will accord some deference to the interpretation and, under a somewhat controversial standard set in *Chevron U.S.A., Inc. v. Natural Resources Defense Council*,[17] allow the agency substantial flexibility in deciding how to apply a standard. When it comes to many laws, what courts must address includes not only statutes, but also administrative regulations issued under the statutes, and administrative determinations of application.

A general question we have already touched on is whether courts should see themselves as "faithful agents" of legislatures or as exercising some independent authority. Of course, if a statute is unconstitutional judges are exerting an independent authority, but what of how they continue to apply a statute? Two points are notable here. Often, we will have no clear line between how the meaning of a provision should be understood and the overriding of that meaning. One example of this is when an overall purpose is taken to counter the ordinary sense of words. For example, in the case of "defendants" being able to preclude potentially prejudicial testimony,[18] did the meaning of "defendants" here exclude civil defendants or did the inclusive meaning give way to obvious considerations of fairness, namely that civil defendants should not receive such a privilege denied to civil plaintiffs? In instances such as this, it is not really productive to ask if judges are actually being faithful to the meaning of words; the focus should be on whether what they are doing is justified.

The second point is that the division between faithful agency and independent authority becomes much more complex as time passes. In respect to "faithfulness," should it be to the original enactors or include what most modern legislators would almost certainly see as a better understanding or application? Even if one focuses on original enactors decades ago, judges might ask how the enactors wanted, or would want, their statute to be interpreted in light of changing conditions and values. All this generates the absence for some situations of a clear distinction between faithful agency and independent action. Again, we need not to be too caught up in this theoretical distinction. It is better to ask what in our system is fairest and most desirable when judges deal with recently enacted and long-standing laws.

V. CONSTITUTIONAL LAWS

When we turn to the United States Constitution, the relevance of the passage of time and of fundamental practices and values that have changed are much more important than with typical statutes. In respect to constitutional interpretation, it helps to recognize a distinction that could be seen as important, but is hardly clear at the edges. One might regard the application of open-ended provisions as different from whether provisions themselves should be maintained.

An illustration of the application of an open-ended provision would be whether a certain communication counts as "speech" protected by the First Amendment. Another example is whether one should see the coverage of the equal protection clause of the Fourteenth Amendment as now properly providing equality for women, given modern values. These shifts in application might be seen as faithful to what the clauses themselves mean, and may have meant in a core sense when enacted, even if applications were then seen as narrower. Matters are less simple if one asks about striking down an application of a form of capital punishment still maintained in most states, and more fundamentally, the use of the Fourteenth Amendment's due process clause to make most of the Bill of Rights applicable to states. The Eighth Amendment covers punishments that are "cruel and unusual." Could invalidation of widespread practices be seen as a disregard of "unusual"? And, if the due process clause was initially seen as covering procedure, is application to substantive laws especially a disregard for what the terms mean? In both these instances, the Supreme Court or other judges are not totally abandoning a provision, but they are treating it in a way that reaches beyond open-ended application to alter its effective meaning.

Since most of the issues in the United States involve open-ended provisions or the understanding of vague standards, I shall concentrate on those. Most of the reasons for accepting evolution in application are fairly obvious. The Constitution was adopted 227 years prior to 2018. This makes it much harder to determine original intentions and understandings. Even the crucial Fourteenth Amendment, with its equal protection clause and, according to Supreme Court construction, its inclusions of most of the Bill of Rights against the states, was proposed 153 years ago. With some exceptions, this makes it much harder to determine relevant reader understanding and adopter intentions than is true with recent statutes. A second key point is the open-endedness of many provisions, including the formulation of many of the protections of individual rights in the Bill of Rights.

Two related factors are that our Constitution is very hard to amend, and it carries great symbolic significance. If the courts simply stuck with original understanding, it is likely that in many crucial respects that would simply fail to conform to modern values, such as equality of women. And if, somehow, amendments became much more frequent, this could undermine the document's symbolic power. All these present strong reasons for judges not simply to try to apply understood coverage at the time provisions were adopted. With these generalizations, we can now look at more detailed considerations.

It helps first to think about the kinds of changes over time. One evident change is new technologies and developing social environments. Clearly as new techniques to torture convicted criminals develop, these could constitute "cruel and unusual" punishment under the Eighth Amendment even if unconceived at the time of adoption. A somewhat more complex example involves "unreasonable search" under the Fourth Amendment, which says that warrants can be issued only upon "probable cause." Although I do believe that at any stage of history, the seriousness of a possible crime could make a difference, let us suppose that the original understanding was that searches generally should take place only if the likelihood of damning evidence was more probable than not. Since that stage of history, major cities have grown hugely in their populations, and one form of dangerous behavior is thefts and assaults carried out on the street by people who can quickly leave the scene. Of course, another modern concern is possible terrorist acts. Should police be able to stop suspects and physically examine them to some degree on less than "probable cause"? The judicial resolution is to allow "stop and frisk" on a lower probability than would be required for an ordinary search within a house. Although we have had a concern that in at least some cities police have engaged in racial discrimination in their stops,[19] the basic notion that less probability is needed here makes sense.

A rather different factor is how society is organized. An obvious change is that with developing technology of various sorts, the essential division between different parts of the country has greatly reduced itself. This could clearly bear on what one thinks the federal government should be able to do and what should be limited to the choices of individual states.

A more interesting example involves controversy over the Second Amendment, which reads, "A well regulated Militia, being necessary to the security of a free State, the right of the people to keep and bear Arms, shall not be infringed."[20] Given that the possession of weapons in one's home has virtually nothing to do now with military service, should that nevertheless be seen as protected by the Constitution? In 2008, the Supreme Court concluded yes in the controversial case of *District of Columbia v. Heller*.[21] The majority downplayed the legal significance of a "well regulated Militia." The four dissenters disagreed, believing that the reason to confer this particular individual right against legislative restraint no longer existed.

A different response to changed organization was in *Miranda v. Arizona*.[22] Given the active modern role of police in enforcing the law, including their questioning of suspects, the Supreme Court held that to protect against self-incrimination, officials including police had to provide an explicit warning to persons they would question if they wanted responses to be available as evidence. This was not anything close to a particular understanding when the Fifth Amendment was adopted.

The third kind of basic change involves a shift in underlying values. The original Constitution implicitly recognized that slavery existed in many states, and when the Fourteenth Amendment was adopted, women definitely did not have equal rights, including a right to vote. It would be conceivable for courts to simply adhere to rights as originally perceived and leave any expansion by statutes or within the Constitution up to legislatures, but, of course, that is not what the Supreme Court has actually done. Another illustration of changes in perceptions concerns acceptable punishments. At our founding, capital punishment was authorized for many ordinary crimes such as thefts and sexual relations between those of the same gender. Both the examples of restricting capital punishment and expanding rights of equality represent the interpretation of open-ended provisions to confer rights in light of modern values rather than sticking to original understandings of coverage.

The application of a "rational basis" test for most forms of economic regulation, challenged by some as violating the Constitution, can be seen as involving a combination of shifts. Most obviously, technology regarding our economic life has developed greatly since the original Constitution. This makes increased government involvement, both in terms of regulation and rights protection, such as minimum wages, a natural consequence. Even if basic individual rights regarding things such as hours worked were perceived as outside government interference in the eighteenth century, that is no longer so. Thus, we can see allowing regulation under the "rational basis" test as reflecting both technological development and a reduced sense of individual rights in this domain.

Another relevant consideration has been the effective role of the Supreme Court. The Court once treated cases as ordinary appeals. But when this jurisdiction led to many more cases than the Court could handle per term, shifts were made so that its jurisdiction is now discretionary. It chooses what to review, and its choice depends mainly on whether a case raises an important issue, not whether on balance the decision below was probably the right one. Its main function is to guide the law, not simply to decide if a result is correct. For both the Supreme Court and lower courts to defer to what other officials have decided fits well with this dominant role.[23]

Having looked at some general differences between our Constitution and most statutes and the basic relations between them, we will explore more specific complications that bear on actual and proper interpretations of provisions. As mentioned in the prior chapter, a distinction between intentions and reader understanding is much harder to draw if the focus is on more than two centuries ago. We now have little evidence of how most people understood things other than what the enactors communicated they were doing and what were common practices of the time.

A number of related points concern what should count. A primary basis for focusing on reader understanding is the notion that what it is fair to demand of citizens depends on what they understand as legal requirements and as granted rights. For this concern, what citizens now perceive matters much more than what others who died long ago understood. It follows that insofar as original meaning and relevant applications should either control or carry significant weight, the intentions of enactors should now matter more for most of the Constitution than what was reader understanding so long ago. Of course, present reader understanding should be important, but with many provisions that will depend as much, or more, on previous Supreme Court decisions than on the text itself.

With virtually all kinds of textual restraints, an important issue, which we have looked at in Chapter 1, is the comparative importance of specific applications that seem to fit both the language and intentions, in relation to broader principles and purposes captured by a provision. As time goes by, especially with language that is open-ended, it makes sense to give increasing importance to the broader objectives in relation to perceived applications. Although with other legal texts, broader aspects of the body of law can matter; a special feature of our Constitution is that what the entire document does can count for how a particular provision should be interpreted.

Somewhat related to this point is how judges should determine issues of rights and justice that are left open to resolution by the Constitution itself. It is often conceived that judges are called upon to make moral judgments in difficult cases, but they should be relying mainly on community morality, not their personal moral convictions. As we shall explore in later chapters, saying what exactly counts as the relevant community morality is far from simple; but, as with interpreting what the document itself entails, the general premises of community morality should generally count for more than specific applications if these are in conflict. Especially when one thinks of rights of those in minorities, it should matter more whether what they are claiming fits with broad cultural norms rather than what a majority of people may or may not accept at this particular time. One reason for this is the concern that actual legislators may make concessions to the interests or prejudices of dominant majorities.

Related to these observations just made, we need to recognize that much may depend on the kind of provision involved. If the issue concerns the respective powers of the federal and state governments, or branches of the federal government, judges might conclude that the understanding of relevant officials matters a lot more than that of ordinary citizens; but if the concerns are what political advocacy is protected speech or what forms of religious exercise are protected rights, the sense of ordinary people is highly important. The nature of a provision affects the proper strategy of application.

I have noted earlier that a serious originalist needs to take into account what were originally conceived as proper methods of interpretation. Although this is hardly simple to determine, and it can be arguable just whose views should count, courts at the time of the Constitution, based partly on British common law, saw interpretation as somewhat flexible over time, rather than a rigorous adherence to statutory language and common law decisions. A genuine originalist needs to take this into account, especially if we are talking about provisions that are open-ended rather than highly specific. If judges were really trying to be faithful to this aspect of original understanding, an obvious implication would be that approaches to interpretation should vary somewhat depending on when a provision was adopted. This could be very complicated, requiring numerous different approaches depending on dates of enactment. I am not aware of any "originalist" who actually adopts this position.

What I have just observed, as well as considerations about a viable approach to applications, generates serious concerns about how the major parts of the Bill of Rights should apply to what the state and federal governments do. The Supreme Court has decided that the Fourteenth Amendment adopted after the Civil War has rendered the crucial provisions of the Bill of Rights, which initially applied only to the federal government, as controlling the states as well. How does this bear on actual coverage?

If we focus on understanding of coverage at the time of adoption, this itself would vary for the coverage of many important particular provisions. How far controversial speech was conceived as protected and what could amount to "cruel and unusual punishment" almost certainly developed over time. A strict originalist would need to ask whether a complaint is being raised against the federal government or a state, and the outcome of a case could depend on that, since, given differences in understanding between 1791 and 1865, the result could rest on which government was the defendant. Apart from the basic complexity of this, the consequence would be at odds with a basic value of a federal system. Since the ideas of individual rights had already expanded to a degree between the Bill of Rights and the Fourteenth Amendment, the federal government would be less restricted than states. In a federal system, when it comes to individual rights, if any governments should have more power to infringe, they should be those of individual states, which would then make various choices. To allow the federal government to undermine freedom of speech more that any state does not make practical sense.

A minor reason not to be a genuine originalist about our Constitution is that when it was adopted, slaves, women, and a fair number of free men did not have a right to vote. One could easily argue that representatives who formed the Constitution and the Bill of Rights were not actually fairly standing for our whole population.

A more complex consequence of sticking to original understanding is one whose practical significance is much harder to determine. This concerns standards of interpretation themselves. If judges really tried to be faithful to how standards were conceived at the time of enactment, they would employ somewhat different interpretive approaches for claims of free speech and free exercise of religion depending on whether the claim was against the federal or a state government. More broadly, for any provision now in the Constitution, they would employ the approach generally accepted when a provision was adopted. Realistically, it is not feasible to ask judges to shift their approaches to constitutional analysis on this basis. Doing so would be much more difficult than responding to a provision in an individual contract that provides specific guidance about how it should be interpreted.

One consequence of all this is that at least for open-ended provisions we have no simple single standard of interpretation that is being used or that should be used. We need to recognize that the complications of complying with instructions over time are not limited to the law. If a single parent has to leave for six months and gives instructions to her brother on how to take care of her son Samuel, the brother may find out over time that some specific instructions, such as sugar in a needed diet, are at odds with general purposes and that other instructions really do not fit Samuel's character. We human beings have no clearly defined ordering that tells us when the specific directions should be disregarded or construed in a way probably at odds with the instructor's intentions. Constitutional law does have some distinctive complexities, and, of course, prior decisions count for a lot, but in the significance of multiple bases for judgments and no clear ordering that applies across the board, this area of law is not so different from the rest of our lives.

One significant feature of how judges should interpret provisions is that they need to take into account what they and others can actually determine. To take a notable example that actually cut back on constitutional free exercise rights, in *Employment Division v. Smith*,[24] the Supreme Court ruled that if a law, such as a bar on the use of peyote, was cast generally and was not designed to attack religious practices, no one had a free exercise right to violate it. A central ground in Justice Scalia's opinion for the Court was that it was too hard to determine with such laws when a genuine religious practice was being impaired.

Tied to some of these various considerations is the question of the appropriate degree of judicial deference to other branches of government. If the status of a practice is arguable, should judges accept what other officials have determined? This is one of the aspects in which the kind of provision matters. If it concerns relations between Congress and the president, or federal and state governments, and the branches involved are themselves not in disagreement, the reason for deference is fairly strong, and sometimes has even risen to a "political question" doctrine, under which the judges simply accept what the other branches have resolved. If the issue is a claim that officials have impaired important individual rights, any basis for deference is much weaker, since a crucial basis for constitutional rights is a concern that government officials will have inclinations to impair them. As we have seen, whether economic regulation genuinely involves individual rights is an important question about the "rational basis" test—whether it should exist, and how it should be applied? In respect to deference, judges appropriately accord more to Congress than to legislatures and executives within states that are claimed to violate national rights.

An important question about interpreting the Constitution is how much weight to give precedents. In our system, these are very important in this area as well as others. When one asks about the relation between hate speech and freedom of speech, for any practical purpose, one looks at Supreme Court cases, not some original understanding. This significance is supported both by desirable stability and fair notice within a legal system, and by what public understanding of a provision will be at any particular time. This, of course, is one aspect of our law that differs from informal communications and relations.

The status of precedents provides the most important example of differences among courts that can also matter in other respects. Most discussions of constitutional interpretation concern what the Supreme Court has decided or will decide. Should judges in courts of appeals and district courts do the same thing? With precedents, the answer clearly is that a court that has itself laid down a precedent has more room to revoke or overturn it than a court below it. A federal district court judge should not reject a Supreme Court precedent even if he thinks that the Supreme Court should overrule it.

A rather different question about the status of various courts is how far judges should reach beyond resolving individual cases and set more general standards. An example here is *Miranda v. Arizona*,[25] in which the Supreme Court formulated a specific warning that police must give suspects if evidence is to be used of what the suspects say. Here, as with overriding, this is generally more appropriate for the highest court in a jurisdiction, including a state supreme court regarding state law, than for lower courts. I am not suggesting that judges in lower courts should never suggest such rules, but they will not have the authority to effectively make them binding across the board.

A final concern is how candid judicial opinions should be about the bases for decisions. This concern exists across the board, but it carries the greatest weight in constitutional decisions, especially those of the Supreme Court. Two obstacles are crucial here. The first is that it is desirable to have majority opinions in the mostly difficult cases the Court chooses to review. Given the need to have five Supreme Court justices to sign on in order to achieve these, and given the inevitability that there will be some disagreement among them about what matters and how much, we cannot expect such a majority opinion to accurately represent everyone's actual views. The second obstacle is a bit more arguable.

Judges generally write opinions to indicate that the balance of reasons strongly supports their result. We rarely see an opinion, even an individual opinion, which indicates that the arguments on each side are evenly balanced and that a judge thinks her position is only slightly stronger than the opposing view. Whether judges should be more candid about the weight of arguments is debatable. This might better reveal what matters and how much. But, would it be disturbing for parties to a case and others if it were made evident that in the judges' minds the arguments were about equally strong and their conclusion was definitely debatable? That kind of candor might also undermine to a degree the extent to which decisions by higher courts help to set the law that then is in practice.

When we put many of these points together we can identify four solid reasons why most judges are not, and should not be, rigorously originalist about methods of interpretation. The most obvious is our limited insight concerning how Constitution makers themselves and others at the time believed the original document should be interpreted. A second is the difficulty of ascertaining for each period of amendment just how interpretation was mainly conceived. Together, these constitute a third difficulty: the near unworkability of an original approach for interpretation for the entire modern document. The fourth reason against rigorous originalism here is that an argument that those who adopted provisions more than a century ago have claims of authority over the process of interpretation of modern judges is itself weak.

We have seen in this examination of the Constitution, and how judges should approach it, that in some respects, such as the related roles of readers and enactors, some questions are not so different from those for statutes and contracts. But in many respects, including the more complex way its provisions are adopted, the symbolic significance of the document, the difficulty of amendment, and the open-ended character of many key phrases, especially those involving basic individual rights, the Constitution raises special questions and yields some distinctive answers regarding the passage of time.

VI. COMMON LAW

I shall say just a few words about an aspect of our system that does not exist in civil law systems such as France and Italy. That is the common law, which is created by courts themselves. As was historically true in England, a good bit of the law concerning things such as contracts was developed in this way, and at an earlier time even a fair amount of criminal law was so created. In the interesting case of *State v. Bradbury*,[26] the Maine Supreme Court in 1939 decided that an old man was properly indicted for burning the body of his deceased sister in a furnace in his house's basement. This was taken as an indecent disposal of her body at odds with the "feelings and the interests of the living."[27] The opinion quotes Judge Holmes that what counts for such classifications are "the actual feelings and demands of the community."[28] It also notes that the common law is not fixed and inflexible as a statute, but is based on elementary principles that lead to expansion with the progress of society and changes in matters such as trade and commerce.

The common law has always had a much lesser role in federal law than the law of states dealing with areas such as torts and contracts, and in most states it is now irrelevant for criminal law, since these duties must be defined by legislation. But common law still has an important role in our system as a whole.

As the *Bradbury* case illustrates, a decision based on the common law reaches a result about a particular situation, but also typically includes a broader announced principle that will extend to other situations. When novel circumstances arise, the contention can be that they are covered by existing principles or are similar enough so that reasoning by analogy should reach them. In brief, the common law rests largely on judicial assessments of community morality and the force of existing precedents. As with many subjects in constitutional law, exactly what counts as community morality and what to do if outlooks on specific questions do not fit with broader principles is hardly clear and precise. To return to *Bradbury*, if all the brother was trying to do was to dispose of the body of his dead sister, why should the emotional reactions of other people to this substitute for burying outweigh the privilege of a reasonable person to choose the technique that best fit his convictions and inclinations? One could easily argue that the opinion really goes too far in limiting behavior; no clear principle really dictates the result, at least if we put aside a possible concern (not mentioned) that allowing such actions might help people conceal their having taken a relative's life.

Two points about the role of precedents are important. The first is that as with other subjects, when higher courts set precedents, judges in courts below them should be, and are, much more hesitant to overturn an established rule than the courts that have laid them down. The second point has more to do with this particular area of law. Given the connection of common law to community morality and to particular practices, the willingness of courts to deviate from, or directly override, precedents with the passage of time is somewhat greater than in many other areas. Of course, legislatures can override common law precedents with statutory law, and one could argue that this should constitute a reason for judges themselves to be hesitant to do so; but it is not a premise of our system that legislators are paying a good bit of attention to all this and that judges should therefore leave things where they stand.

In summary, in contrast to many other aspects of law, such as wills, contracts, statutes, and constitutions, we have here no basic texts that judges are called upon to respect and construe. But as an area of the law, common law does partly determine how some texts, such as contracts, will be understood, and for general approaches to interpretation over time, it is fairly flexible in a way that is also true for open-ended provisions of the Constitution.

VII. CONCLUSION

This chapter has explored a range of considerations that bear on how judges do, and should, respond to changing conditions and to legal texts that are at odds with important values. The answers here, as with many questions about judicial interpretation, are far from simple. They depend greatly on what kind of legal standard is involved so, even if one focuses on a particular statutory or constitutional provision, or something else, multiple factors may play a role, and their relative weight can be arguable.

3

Conceptualization as It Relates to Actual and Recommended Practices

I. INTRODUCTION

In this chapter, we explore various conceptualizations of what judges do and should do, and how these relate to understandings and evaluations. Are judges interpreting a document or adding to or revising its content? Are they applying the law or creating law? Are they being "faithful" to the Constitution, statutes, and contracts, or reaching beyond them to exercise independent power?

The chapter has a basic theme, relying largely on examples mentioned in the first two chapters. The theme is that these conceptualizations, to a large degree, do help us to understand the significant differences between what judges typically do and don't do, and also between what they should do and should not do. But unfortunately, these categorizations do not tell us exactly what judges do and whether their actions are warranted.

There are two difficulties. The first is that like most moral and political concepts, the edges of coverage are not themselves precise, so we have numerous borderline instances of difficult cases for which it is arguable exactly how a particular strategy of resolution fits. The second problem directly consider how judges should treat this, not get completely tied up in whether it amounts to a revision. Again, whichever approach judges take, one may or may not perceive that as authorized by the general law. Of course, in respect to a good bit of broader law relating to contracts and wills, its creation has been by judges and the common law, not legislatures. If no existing precedents govern or point toward a result, it is a bit artificial to see a common law decision as being based on preexisting law.

When we turn to contracts, what is normally required is carrying out their terms. That is a clear application. How are we to characterize what takes place if doing so is grossly unfair or at odds with what the contracting parties conceived? When rooms that had been rented for a day or so to watch the king's coronation parade had lost their effective value because the parade had been cancelled, judges did not require remaining payments.[5] This could be seen as faithful to the overall sense of the contract—a kind of application or intended non-application—although it deviated from specific terms. The result was supported by the overall law of how contracts should be treated.

In other situations, the literal terms may point in one direction but the apparent purposes in another. In one of these cases, the divorcing husband agreed to pay his wife $1,200 a year for support of their son until he entered college.[6] The son was drafted into the military after high school. Did the former husband need to pay for the years in the military? In another case, the agreement was to sell property to a neighbor according to double the value set by an official agency.[7] The agency had set a value far, far below its responsibility to specify half of the market value. In the support payment case, the court, assuming that the parents conceived the son would go directly to college from high school, did not require payment for his time in military service. In the property dispute, the owner was compelled to sell at about a quarter of actual market value because this fit the specifications of the contract.

What both these cases raise is how to characterize what judges do when they must decide whether to apply the specific terms of a contract or fulfill its broader purposes, and the answer is not as clear as it was for the rooms to be rented to watch the coronation parade. The terms of the contracts themselves do not provide a decisive answer. One could say that for the contract that required payment to support the son, the court decided not to apply its terms in order to do what was fair; but one might instead say the court was actually applying the contract according to a reasonable understanding of what it really entailed. The court that required the sale of property at a price that was incredibly low could be seen as simply applying the contract's terms or as actually deviating from what the contract was really about because the agency had failed to perform its function. My basic point about all this is that these various conceptualizations may help us to understand what was going on, but cannot by themselves tell us how the judges should approach cases when these competing considerations are in play. For that, we need to ask questions concerning fairness to contract makers, what is feasible for judges to determine without too great a cost of resources, and what is desirable for our system as a whole.

A final contracts situation is one in which a term can be understood in two different ways, and each is equally plausible. My hypothetical example of working during the "summer" fits that. A court might decide that if two different understandings are both quite reasonable, it should pick the more general literal usage or the usage that is more common for students who work during their summer vacation; or it might decide that if the understandings are different and about equally reasonable, no contract existed. If it chooses one meaning over the other, we can say it is merely applying the contract as best it can or that it is supplementing the contract by filling in a standard that the contract itself does not really resolve. Again, these competing conceptualizations do not themselves really tell us what a court has done or should do.

When we turn to statutes and the Constitution, we can identify more troubling and debatable questions. I shall start with statutes and their relation to the Constitution. If a statute is plainly unconstitutional the court is obviously not applying it but is applying higher law, as it would if a contract or a will violated a statute. A more difficult question I have mentioned is how to conceptualize a court relying on constitutional values to conceive a statute in a way that is intrinsically different from its apparent content.

Within our system, statutes are subject to constitutional requirements. If we put aside the political question doctrine for certain relations between branches of government, courts will declare clear constitutional violations to be so and will hold such statutes or particular provisions to be invalid. In these situations, judges are applying a higher law to hold invalid what would otherwise be law.

A somewhat different situation exists when a statute could plausibly be interpreted in each of two ways, only one of which is constitutional. Courts would accord it that content. This can be perceived effectively as applying the statute in the only way that works according to higher law. Just how to characterize things becomes a bit more difficult if the most plausible reading is unconstitutional and the judges choose an alternative reading that they are willing to sustain. We can see this in the two cases, *Seeger* and *Welsh*, interpreting the Draft Act to include people who were not religious believers in any ordinary sense.[8] That understanding, which was at odds with the plain terms of the law itself and with dominant legislative intentions to counter earlier cases that reached a more generous conclusion about a vaguer version of the statute, was not simply applying the existing statute in any straightforward sense. Was the Court making the law? One could argue that if the more plausible reading would be unconstitutional, this was really an attempt to do the best the justices could to make the statute effective, which therefore didn't amount to their making the law. On the other hand, if judges are self-consciously not treating the statute according to its terms and what legislators intended to do, one might characterize this as a form of their effectively *making* law, even if they are responsive to constitutional limits. This characterization would be especially plausible if judges could not really determine whether Congress would prefer this strained reading to invalidation of the statute. As I have noted, in his concurrence in *Welsh*, Justice Harlan expressed his view that Congress had drawn an unconstitutional line, but joined the granting of the exemption on the basis that members of Congress would prefer the broader coverage to invalidation of the whole statute.

As with many other examples, the possibilities of how one classifies such strained readings in various ways are not what really matters. What is crucial is whether in our system this is the appropriate way for judges to behave, namely in order to sustain its constitutionality, to read a particular statute in a way that does not meet ordinary criteria.

Similar questions arise if judges divert from the most plausible reading of a statute to avoid constitutional doubts, even if they are not themselves sure, or do not make clear, whether the alternative reading would actually be unconstitutional. Here the "higher law" is not exactly dictating the result because the more plausible version of the statute *might* survive constitutional attack. One could see this as a kind of rejection of what Congress has actually done without a direct reliance on a higher law. That could be cast as a version of judges "making law." But one might instead say that since Congress could re-enact the law more specifically in a way that would require resolution of the constitutional issue, this judicial practice is actually grounded in an overall concession to Congress to avoid troubling constitutional issues about statutes when possible. This could be seen as a construction that fits the overall objectives of Congress, if not the specific understanding of text and the intentions in this situation. Again, what really matters is whether this is a desirable judicial approach.

A slightly different circumstance is when each of two plausible readings would definitely be sustainable constitutionally, but one of the two readings seems to fit better with constitutional values. We can imagine a statute cast neutrally but the most straightforward reading would be likely to be more advantageous for a dominant race, or men over women, or one religious denomination over others. If judges are definitely not applying the higher law but relying on its values to construe such a statute in a less plausible form, it is a bit harder to say they are merely applying law rather than making it; but one could respond that relying on those values is part of what the higher law should be conceived as influencing, and this could be seen as a kind of remote dimension of application. What really matters is what judges should be doing in these circumstances.

Closely related to much of the prior discussion is whether judges should see themselves as "faithful agents" of Congress or as sometimes "independent legislators." In many of the circumstances we have just looked at, it is extremely hard to say what a "faithful agent" would do. Does that entail being "faithful" in construing the most evident meaning if that would be clearly unconstitutional, possibly unconstitutional, or definitely constitutional but in tension with constitutional values? Exactly how one would construe "faithful agency" would itself depend on a less than simple judgment about the relation between legislators and judges. And, as noted in other contexts, much might depend here on how simple it would be to re-enact pieces of legislation that have been judicially treated in a way that does not best fit direct legislative aims.

Having explored the relation to the Constitution, we will now consider more simple questions of understanding statutory language. Before turning to illustrations of specific language, we can ask about the status of any doctrine that statutes should generally be understood to fit with other statutory provisions, and governing aspects of the common law. Especially since dominant political parties and legislative members shift over time, one might see this as generating failures to apply the laws in a way that is faithful to the groups that enacted them. But what counts as "the law" here? One might argue that despite their various positions on specific subjects, legislators would generally subscribe to the aspiration for consistency among statutes in situations in which the contrary is not clearly dictated by the individual texts, and they might welcome the continuing broader influence over time of laws they have enacted. Thus, their broader intent *might* concede some qualifications about the specific coverage of texts they have enacted. As with various examples involving constitutional rights and values, one could urge that the judges who engage in this practice are failing to apply adopted laws, and instead are making law, or that they are applying the law in a broader sense. Similarly, this could be seen as acting independently or as a form of "faithful agency" toward Congress as broadly conceived.

How should we understand more straightforward examples in which judges do not apply statutory terms in accord with their literal language? Sometimes these are definitely aspects of applying the law, and at other times one might urge that judges are making law. The latter situations could occur when judges definitely choose a less plausible reading or when they choose between competing plausible readings based on reasons not drawn from the statute itself.

Let us start with clear deviations from literal terms. I mentioned the time I was directed by a police officer to pull over to the side of the street, and he rewarded me by giving me a parking ticket rather than a speeding ticket. A sign that says, "No Parking" cannot plausibly be read to cover a situation in which you are directed by a police officer to park your car so that he can talk to you. An actual Supreme Court case that was unanimous against a literal reading involved a provision that gave "defendants" a right to preclude prejudicial testimony.[9] While it was appropriate to give a criminal defendant such a right that was not available to a prosecutor, treating civil defendants differently from civil plaintiffs really had no basis. Thus, "defendants" here was limited to those in criminal cases. In situations like this, we can speak of judges as applying the law, since they are reading the statute in the only way that makes sense and fits with legislative intentions, although they are departing from literal linguistic coverage.

In some other situations, broader values come into play for how language is understood. In the example of the teenager who killed his grandfather,[10] the relevant statute that covered wills was treated as barring his receiving benefits although it contained no specific limitation. The logic was that people cannot be rewarded for criminal behavior. If we looked just at the language of the law regarding wills, we might say the court "created" law by making an exception, but we could also say that this was a fair application of the law in general because, given the absence of a provision directly on point, the statute was interpreted to conform to underlying principles aimed at discouraging criminal behavior and refusing to reward those who engage in it. This circumstance is not so different from judges relying on constitutional values in deciding how a statute is to be taken even when the approach they reject would not be actually unconstitutional. In fact, when judges rest largely on underlying values of the legal system, it is often unclear whether these plausibly count as constitutional or not. As with other illustrations, what matters is whether and when judges should use this technique, not whether it constitutes an example of "applying" or "making" law, or a combination.

What of the situations in which the statutory language is genuinely unclear in context? I have suggested that in most locations "No sleeping" in a railroad station would not cover delayed passengers who take brief naps while sitting and waiting, but in other locations the understood purposes behind the rule might cover these naps. What if in a particular instance it was genuinely debatable how broad the coverage should be taken to be? One could easily say that the judges who decide this are effectively making law on a subject left open by the legislation itself. But if one believes that the judges are, or should be drawing from broader aspects of the law, one might conclude that they are really only applying the law in general. For this, a good bit depends on what one counts as "the law," a subject we shall cover below.

An actual case that included two plausible views of coverage was whether "uses or carries a firearm," which increased potential penalties, reached purchasing a drug in exchange for a weapon.[11] Justice Scalia dissenting, said no because "using" a weapon ordinarily means actually employing it to accomplish what a weapon can do. The Court's majority ruled that employing it to buy something did count as a relevant "use." As I have noted, the fact that sellers of drugs might be receiving weapons from customers may or may not be seen as a relevant concern about general dangers. But whether that was something that members of Congress had in mind was not clear. If we perceive both the majority's and Scalia's positions as plausible, how would we characterize what the majority did or what the Court would have done if the other justices had accepted Scalia's view? We can see both the actual majority and Justice Scalia as applying the statute as they perceived it. Suppose we could characterize the majority's position as giving weight to what made practical sense, whereas Justice Scalia argued that the ordinary sense of language should be crucial. Each side might see the other as "making law" by deviating from the proper approach, whereas both sides would regard themselves as simply applying the law. Of course, the crucial question is what approach should actually be taken to this kind of language in this context.

I have not addressed statutes that are open-ended in their language and effectively call for executive officials and judges to determine what they should be taken to cover. The considerations here are similar to those that concern open-ended constitutional provisions, which we will address shortly.

The questions about judges creating or applying law are most pervasive and vital when it comes to the Constitution. As with statutes and contracts, some constitutional provisions have clear applications, such as the age one needs to be in order to become president, and the procedures necessary to adopt federal law. But many provisions, especially those concerning individual rights, are open-ended, and therefore indecisive about exactly what they cover. What are judges doing when they fill in the terms of such provisions by determining whether a law or practice does or does not deny freedom of speech, cruel and unusual punishment, or equal protection? This is complicated in several ways.

Let us start with two positions. One is that judges should simply stick with the original understanding at the time of enactment about what was covered and what was not. A competing position or various competing positions say that judges must make more complex judgments about what is now covered by constitutional protection, which may well include deviations from original understanding. A justice who chooses to stick with original understanding might claim that he is applying the law rather than making law, whereas justices taking a more flexible approach are making the law. Even this is not simple. As emphasized in the majority opinion creating a constitutional protection for same-sex marriage,[12] the founders may have endorsed a flexibility that responds to developing values over time. On that understanding, the flexible approach is a more faithful application of the actual law than complete rigidity, which itself can then be seen as a kind of "making" of law that really deviates from what the constitution-makers enacted.

Suppose we accept a somewhat flexible approach to such things as restraints on capital punishment, equality of women to men, and of gay individuals to heterosexual ones. How should judges decide what is now covered by constitutional protections? Should they give weight to changes in other aspects of the law, such as statutes authorizing same-sex marriage, to community morality, to their own moral judgments, or some combination of these? If the primary reliance was on their own moral judgments, this could easily be seen as judges making law; but what of other aspects of law and community morality? Even if reliance on constitutional values is a kind of higher law in relation to statutes, does lower law affect the proper content of constitutional law, or is this a form of judicial creation? About community morality, we have subtle questions concerning what should count: general propositions such as human equality, or more particular beliefs, such as whether marriage should include gay couples? If one thinks that in some complex way the law provides an answer to these questions, one might contend that even when justices rely on community morality to create constitutional rights, the Supreme Court is really "applying" the law. But one might well see the Court's decision protecting same-sex marriage as creating new constitutional law. The important question is not whether this is best characterized as application, or creation, or as a kind of combination, but whether it is appropriate for the Court to be doing it.

If the Supreme Court makes a decision that clearly reaches beyond both an original understanding of actual practices and of proper methods of interpretation, this could well be seen as the most obvious example of making law; but even here one might claim that the entire body of constitutional law has now developed to render this appropriate. When we put all these observations together, we can conclude that there are many, many instances in which judges simply "apply" the law to clear or disputed factual circumstances. On some unusual occasions, judges seem to "make" law unless "the law" is seen as very extensive and complicated. But in some circumstances, more common for the Supreme Court than other courts, it is hardly clear whether judges are "applying the law" or "making law" or doing a combination of both. My dominant theme is not to reject these categorizations, but to contend that in doubtful circumstances, we need mainly to focus not on which characterization is somehow best but whether the practice is just and desirable. The categorizations themselves cannot simply determine that.

III. DEFERENCE

Having examined the key question about applying and making law, I shall turn to three particular questions about judicial decisions, two of which are aspects of arguable conceptualizations. These two are the place of "precedents" and the significance of "interpretation." I will begin with a simpler question about deference, whose complexities are explored briefly in the preceding chapters. In a fairly wide range of areas, judges will defer to the judgments of other officials about the content of law. This is neither making nor applying the law in any ordinary sense. It is not making the law because judges are accepting what other officials have determined. But neither is it applying the law as the judges perceive the coverage of a governing statute or a constitutional provision. What judges are saying is that if coverage is fairly arguable and some crucial officials have chosen at least a reasonable position, they will accept that in the case before them without determining whether on balance it is the position they themselves would adopt if they decided independently. To take two obvious situations, if a statute sets up standards for administrative officials to employ in setting regulations, judges will often defer to how the officials have read the statute, and if the national and state governments have in effect accepted a kind of allocation of powers, judges will defer to their understanding of what the Constitution requires and allows.

As explained earlier, we can easily perceive two bases for judicial deference. The first is that the officials, called upon to regulate under the law, may be more expert about its content than an ordinary judge. In many aspects of our lives, we defer to those we believe have an understanding superior to our own. The second reason is that deference typically reduces judicial interference with how things operate. If those who are carrying out duties are relying on reasonable interpretations of set standards, judicial acceptance will interfere less with practical operation than a decision that those bodies must abandon their conceptions of guidelines and accept new ones set judicially. This problem has a special quality if the agency operates nationally and the court rejecting its approach has only a limited jurisdiction.

As with our other topics, what really matters is when and to what degree ~~is~~ judicial deference appropriate, not whether such deference deviates from judges themselves applying the law, or by contrast, whether it can be seen as a special form of application of the law that gives appropriate weight to the views of experts, and may follow an underlying general legal proposition that the government should operate smoothly.

IV. PRECEDENTS

An indisputable part of our legal system is that judges follow precedents. As noted earlier, the force of precedents varies; they are more constraining for lower courts than the courts that have set them. But even Supreme Court justices who cast themselves as textualist originalists are generally accepting of well-established precedents. Perhaps the most notable examples are provisions of the Bill of Rights, such as cruel and unusual punishment and freedom of speech, that now go far beyond originally understood coverage and apply to the states as well as federal government. Of course, that acceptance might be defended on the ground that the provisions themselves are open-ended, but another problem about original understanding is evident.

According to Supreme Court doctrine, the due process clause, adopted as part of the Fourteenth Amendment, is what rendered most of the Bill of Rights applicable to the states. As Chapter 1 explains in respect to a critique of the "rational basis" test, the language of "due process," in contrast to a "privileges and immunities" clause that had earlier been interpreted narrowly, repeats language in the Fifth Amendment. It appears clearly to concern procedures, not what is protected from being forbidden. Its judicial use to incorporate most provisions of the Bill of Rights is not the fulfilling in of open-ended language: it is the stretching of language with an apparent content to do something quite different. Nevertheless, all the Supreme Court justices have accepted controlling precedents that rely on the clause to expand to states the protections of the Bill of Rights, an extension that within our federal system in modern times clearly makes practical sense.

One question within our law is how far precedents should be controlling if judges now believe those precedents are misguided. A subtler question is what counts as the force of precedent. The latter question is one aspect of what amounts to applying the law. Two situations are relatively clear. A typical precedent involves a particular fact situation and an announced rule of law. If another case arises in which no argument exists that either its fact situation or relevant considerations are different, then the precedent clearly applies. Reaching a contrary result would involve a departure from it. On the other side, we may have a fact situation that is different and is not covered by the stated rule. The result then is not dictated by the precedent, although its facts or its rule might be the core of analogical reasoning to deal with the new case. There can be disagreement about the analogical force of a particular precedent and about its strength in relation to other considerations, but in such situations a court is not simply applying the law by following the precedent.

Debatable questions concern not only the force precedents should carry in relation to other factors but also what should count as the precedent. Should a precedent be limited to factual situations that are closely similar, or extend to everything that is reached by an announced rule? This disagreement relates to what really counts as "the law" facing judges making a decision. Again, the crucial issue is what judges should take into account, not how much "a precedent" is really about factual circumstances and results, or also announced rules. In practical terms, the definite answer is that both can matter for how one sees a precedent and how far it should constrain judges in subsequent cases.

V. LEGAL INTERPRETATION

That judges typically engage in "legal interpretation" is obvious, but that does not quite tell us exactly what constitutes legal interpretation and how far such interpretation dictates what judges should decide. These are complex questions that have received a good bit of attention in modern scholarship. I shall not explore all this in any depth here, but I will mention a few important points. If all that judges are doing is applying the terms of a will or statute that clearly dictates a particular result, we might say that interpretation is not really necessary. To take a non-legal analogy, if we are subject to instructions that clearly apply—"show up by 11:00 a.m. when our class starts"—we do not conceive of interpretation as being needed. At the other end, if legislators are deciding what law to enact, they are not relying mainly on interpretation of the present law, but on what a desirable law would contain. They may, of course, be somewhat restrained by what they see as constitutional limits and the coverage of other statutes, and to this extent legal interpretation could influence them.

The more debatable situations involve how judges do and should decide cases in which the existing law does not provide a simple answer. The two important and related conceptual questions for these cases are whether judges should constrain themselves to "legal" interpretation and what actually amounts to that. Suppose for example that the Supreme Court is deciding whether same-sex marriage is constitutionally protected. Does reliance on developing moral outlooks count as an aspect of legal interpretation or something beyond that? And does it matter for that question whether various legal standards themselves authorize such an evaluation? For those who assume that in the separation of powers within our system, judges should limit themselves to legal interpretation, exactly how that is to be conceived makes a big difference. Because the term itself is general without precise edges, a person with this view should not rely heavily on the term itself, but provide reasons that judges should or should not rely on certain kinds of considerations. An alternative approach is to distinguish legal interpretation from the complete category of considerations judges should take into account. For example, in a number of essays Mark Greenberg has proposed that legal interpretation involves the content of the law.[13] This can reach further than the linguistic meaning of legal texts, but does not involve criteria of decisions that extend beyond existing law, unless the law authorizes their use. Professor Greenberg, however, does this without claiming that judges should never reach beyond standards of legal interpretation in arriving at decisions.

When we think about these questions, we can see that it is very important for those who are considering what counts as legal interpretation to ask themselves whether they are considering how judges should see themselves as constrained, or rather how best to classify various criteria judges may appropriately use.

I shall mention two intermediate positions here. One, which is almost certainly correct, is that among forms of legal interpretation, some typically carry more force than others. The second is that even if some reliance on other factors is warranted, "legal interpretation" generally should carry more weight. This possibility makes it hard to distinguish completely what judges should do from what counts as legal interpretation. But the central focus should be on the question of what judges *should* do rather than on what arguably counts as the edges of "legal interpretation."

VI. CONCLUSION

The dominant theme of this chapter is that various conceptualizations can help us to understand what judges do and what they should do, but we must be careful not to give overarching importance to the boundaries of the concepts. Rather, we need to understand how judges do behave and to consider practical reasons that judges should or should not take certain factors into account, and give these factors more or less weight.

4

Differences in Legal Systems

I. INTRODUCTION

This chapter briefly explores how techniques of interpretation may differ among different legal systems. Of course, in the United States, we can have variations within our fifty different states about matters left to state law, such as how local contracts are to be interpreted, but here, my focus is on systems of different countries. These include other English-speaking countries in which common law has played a significant role, and also civil law countries, such as France and Germany, that do not have that core aspect of law.

What can we learn from this exploration? I believe there are at least three basic lessons. The first, and most obvious, is that to some degree forms of interpretation are related to the basic nature of the system. This is most apparent for constitutional law. How courts handle forms of interpretation can depend on how the constitution was adopted, what significance it is assumed to have, and how easy it is to amend. A second thing we may learn is whether things that seem difficult or misguided in our own system are also to be found within others. If we see that the construing of statutes is somewhat troublesome in every jurisdiction, this helps us to understand that many questions are intrinsically difficult, and not simply the product of faulty American understanding. Related to this possibility is a third matter. Grasping what is done in other countries may help us to understand how what takes place in the United States can be improved. We may have not just abstract analysis, but some evidence of what is working or not working elsewhere.

I should emphasize that this comparative analysis is not something on which I am an expert, and a relatively full understanding would require familiarity with what courts do and what scholars write in many different countries. Readers who are particularly interested in this analysis can pursue matters more deeply. My aim is to provide a kind of introduction, and to stress what kinds of questions carry particular importance.

If one wanted to emphasize differences, it might make sense to focus on constitutional law. I shall treat that briefly later in the chapter, instead starting with more common practices, but here I shall just mention that there are huge differences in constitutional formulations, origins, and status. In some countries, a written constitution was added at some point, but without any fundamental change in how the roles of different parts of the government were seen. This is radically different from the United States, in which our original Constitution set out the respective domains of federal and state law fairly soon after the Revolutionary War that freed us from British control. The Fourteenth Amendment after the Civil War created new limits on states, and provided the basic protection for equality in a country in which slavery had been common in many states. As explained in earlier chapters, our Constitution has been very hard to amend, has many key open-ended provisions, and carries substantial symbolic significance. These are reasons to interpret provisions in an evolutionary way that connotes with modern values. In countries where the document is easy to amend and has less symbolic value, we should expect interpretation that is more faithful to original understanding and more rarely employed to overturn legislative choice. Because of the significant differences in the status of actual constitutions, we cannot expect that what is done in one country will often have a decisive lesson for what should be done in another country. And we should be aware that constitutional values can play an important role even in countries in which no written constitution explicitly forbids forms of national legislation.

With these brief observations, I now turn to other forms of law.

II. STATUTORY INTERPRETATION

A key aspect of the judicial role in any liberal democracy is the enforcement of rights and duties enacted by legislators. Since they are elected by the people, legislators have the basic power to decide what the law should do. Whether judges are themselves elected or appointed, their fundamental responsibility is to see that the law is properly understood and carried out. In these respects, liberal democracies are effectively similar to each other. This makes it much harder to perceive the judicial function as fundamentally different in various countries, and also makes it more likely that what is happening in one country can tell us something about what might desirably take place in our own country.

It turns out that what are central concerns in our practices are also present in other systems. How those systems deal with these problems can both help us to understand what viable alternatives are and whether what seems less than ideal in our system is really both undesirable and avoidable. Among the central questions are the proper role of the text and what counts as the crucial text. Another issue is whether the intentions of legislators should count, and if so, how they should be determined.

More subtle related questions are when, and the degree to which, judges should defer to the interpretation and applications of other officials rather than determining on their own what they believe is most appropriate. As Chapters 1 and 2 explain, this practice in the United States is far from clear and is also controversial, raising serious issues about the constitutional role of federal judges.

Another possible consideration is the role of values derived from other statutes, from nonstatutory parts of the law, and from basic premises that are derived from community morality or from the best assessments judges can make. Much of this can be cast as whether judges should be simply "faithful agents" or regard themselves as exercising an independent role; although, as Chapter 3 develops, we need to avoid overly simple characterizations. Of course, if legislation is actually at odds with a forbidding constitutional requirement, the judges are not supposed to be simply faithful agents of the legislature, but I shall not explore that particular circumstance here.

Earlier chapters have examined these various basic considerations as they relate to our system in the United States. Here, the aim is to see what we may learn about other systems and what this might teach us about our own. Some central questions are these. How troublesome is it that we lack practices that are clear and about which judges agree? Could we aim for an approach that is fairly simple and straightforward, as textual originalists may claim? Should judges be self-understanding and candid about what influences them, and to what degree? To some extent, looking at what takes place in other systems can enrich our evaluation of these possibilities.

Before delving into this, I want to note a reality that I have mentioned in earlier chapters, and that extends to systems outside the United States. The focus on how judges understand statutes is typically on appellate courts, often the highest court in a jurisdiction. One cannot accurately generalize about the clarity of statutes by focusing on cases in which those courts write about statutory coverage. As noted in prior chapters, often the coverage of a statute is quite clear. In such instances, such as what constitutes speeding and violates "no parking," people are likely to comply or pay penalties without litigation. And in many actual cases, the crucial issues may be factual about what people have done rather than whether acts of a particular sort were legal or illegal. Even when cases get to appellate courts, the coverage of the law itself may not be genuinely uncertain. The cases that draw attention about interpretation are ones in which the outcome about coverage is not obvious and the right conclusion may well be debatable. It is a serious mistake to generalize from these cases to conclude how uncertain the reach is of statutes across the board. These uncertain applications involve a modest percentage of total situations. I do not mean to imply that greater certainty and clarity would not be desirable, but I do think it is crucial that we understand that generally, what we are looking at are fringe cases, not the core coverage of statutory law.

III. UNDERSTANDING AND APPLYING STATUTES

A key aspect of judicial interpretation is judges' understanding of the content of statutes and how they apply. To a large extent, how this is done is fairly simple and does not differ among various systems. If the language of the statute clearly authorizes or forbids certain behavior, if judges have no reason to suppose that legislators did not want that coverage, and if the application presents no problem in terms of basic values, that is how the statute will be taken. If, as I have explained, the coverage is that simple, it will not result in litigation. Or, if litigation takes place over what a person did or did not do, the statute's application may not be a subject of serious disagreement. Although relatively few cases reach appellate courts and draw the attention of scholars because statutory coverage is debatable, these are far from trivial. How judges apply statutes in such cases is an important question about a legal system, notably the relation between legislators and judges exercising their responsibilities.

It may help at the beginning to note interrelated questions about how judges treat statutes. A central issue we have looked at in Chapter 1 is how far the text should count in relation to the perceived intent of legislators. Should judges try to delve into probable intent apart from what the text itself reveals? Should they actually rely, at least to some extent, on legislative history as well as broader indications of what a law was designed to accomplish? In respect to the "text," we have the questions of how far the comparative emphasis should be on a specific provision, the statute as a whole, and the way the provision and statute connect to the texts of other laws.

For all this, how relevant is the way the legislative process works? This may bear on how well the text reflects what legislators were trying to do and how reliable forms of legislative history, such as committee reports, are likely to be. It can also matter how easy it is for legislators to correct errors made by themselves or by courts.

In terms of description, we can ask what factors judges are taking into account and whether they fail to acknowledge some of these, or do not express their actual weight. The normative corollary is to what extent judges should be carefully reflective and candid about what matters in their decisions. A plain obstacle here is the reality of majority opinions. If various judges have somewhat different views about what counts and how much, these views cannot be simply captured in a single opinion. One might take this reality as pointing in various directions: (1) courts should have fewer majority opinions in difficult cases; (2) judges should aim for fully revealing majority opinions by having simple, straightforward standards of interpretation; (3) we on the outside should just accept that all that is relevant is often not revealed by those opinions. A very important issue about candor that I have noted is whether it is actually desirable for opinions to reveal that judicial conclusions are arguable because both sides are supported by substantial considerations. Of course, that reality is often disclosed by a combination of the majority's presentation with what one or more dissenting opinions urge.

How far are judges aiming for a straightforward approach, and how far should they be? The claimed adherence to "plain meaning" is the most notable of these. As I have indicated, often the meaning really is "plain" in a simple sense, but the vast majority of these circumstances do not end up in debatable appellate cases. Is "plain meaning" a desirable fundamental approach for these cases, and if not, is some other straightforward approach appropriate? Here, we need to ask whether a stated approach that sounds simple, or is taken to be so, or both, really is simple in terms of the considerations that guide judges. When what really happens is somewhat concealed by stated approaches, does this need to be corrected, or is it acceptable?

A central question that relates to all these others is how far judges should be seen and should perceive themselves as independent. I do believe that in all liberal democracies judges are seen as independent in the sense of not being controlled by legislators and executives. But that does not tell us how they should see their function in respect to statutory interpretation. Should they be simply "faithful agents" applying apparent meaning or exercise a degree of independence for the aim of healthy statutory law?

As we have seen, this is not itself a simple division. Of course, if the courts are given authority to enforce constitutional rights, they act "independently" of the legislature if they hold a statute unconstitutional, but that does not tell us how far they should interpret statutes to avoid invalidation. Not adopting the most obvious meaning, which would be unconstitutional, could be seen as an independent choice of a less plausible content; but it could also be seen as faithfully trying to help the legislature accomplish the most it can. If we put aside constitutional issues, we still have no clear line between independence and faithful agency. If the evident sense of a provision is at odds with the broader purposes of a statute, rejecting its apparent meaning could be perceived as a kind of independent review, but it could also be seen as trying "faithfully" to fulfill what the legislature was trying to achieve. Exactly when we reach judicial independence is not simple; but it does clearly reach those circumstances in which courts interpret a law in a way that is at odds with its evident content and the legislature's genuine objectives, because apart from unconstitutionality that coverage strikes judges as contrary to basic values.

With this introduction, we will tackle many of these core inquiries as they are addressed by different systems. A pervasive question is how far differences in treatment among the systems reflect important structural variations in the organizations of government, or differences in legal traditions, or simply seem more or less fortuitous. A normative question about variations among systems is how far they should be tackled in order to provide common techniques. Given transnational and international bodies of law, and the virtual certainty that these will increase in coverage, substantial reasons suggest it would be healthy if the courts in different countries came to treat controlling provisions in roughly the same way. This is especially true for close-knit bodies such as the European Union.

As Chapter 1 explains, a core question in the United States is the relative importance of text versus intent, and the place, if any, of legislative history. I will start with two obvious points. In any system, the statutory text is very important. If it provides a clear answer and no reason presents itself for a different sense, it will and should be followed. But what if a provision's text itself does not yield a definite answer, or seems at odds with other provisions or with some important values? Should judges then consider and give independent weight to legislative intent? Suppose an outcome is possible that stretches explicit language but seems more consistent with what legislators almost certainly meant to do. An American case described in Chapter 1 was the reading of a special right for "defendants" to avoid prejudicial testimony as covering only criminal defendants, since no plausible basis exists for favoring civil defendants over civil plaintiffs.[1] Even the dominant textualist, Justice Scalia, embraced this position, though it fit less well with the literal language than reaching all defendants. I will assume in what follows that in any system judges will engage in such an exercise if the explicit language can be read more expansively or more narrowly and doing so seems clearly called for by both legislative objectives and what makes sense, and does not impair individual rights.

The hard cases are ones in which sticking with the text is not patently at odds with basic objectives, but a substantial argument can be made that the two are in serious tension. Should a study of legislative intent then count, and what should be examined? In respect to this, one can see differences within legal systems that could make a difference. In England, for most of modern history, majority political parties have been effectively responsible for legislation. Their leaders allocated responsibilities for those drafting statutes, and all members in the House of Commons have voted for what their leaders supported. This has yielded three differences between England's typical legislation and that in the United States. The first, which supports less reference to legislative history, is that the text is more likely to be carefully formulated to reach objectives, and has not been qualified to reflect compromises that were concessions to some legislators or to the claims of outside groups with political influence. This suggests less need to reach beyond the text to aspects of legislative history. On the other hand, one might believe that certain aspects of that history, representing the majority party, could have more weight than they do in the United States. Further, it would be much easier to set general standards of what carries weight and how much, since legislative procedures are similar in many situations. These reasons may not themselves provide decisive answers to what should be done, but they do tell us that what takes place and would be best in England does not necessarily provide answers to what should happen in the United States.

For much of English history, judicial reference to parliamentary debates was foreclosed. In 1769 in *Millar v. Taylor*,[2] the Court of the House of Lords established what is regarded as the exclusionary rule, requiring reliance on what was enacted, and not what was discussed. Among the reasons given over history were that the statutes are publicly accessible and can be understood, and that the search for relevant legislative materials can often be time-consuming and fruitless. In the late twentieth century, criticism was made of the exclusionary rule, and in the 1992 decision of *Pepper v. Hart*,[3] the House of Lords qualified the exclusionary rule when determining what tax benefits teachers at a private school had to pay when their children were afforded a much lower tuition than other students. The majority opinion stated that legislative history could be considered under three conditions; the provision being construed must be ambiguous, unclear, or lead to absurd result; only statements made in Parliament by a minister or promoter of a bill could be considered; and those statements had to be unequivocal. The concern about increasing the costs of litigation was raised by the dissenting opinion.

This approach has subsequently been criticized for raising costs, for providing little help in resolving disputes, and for possibly even being unconstitutional by affording the Minister the power to do what is reserved for the legislature. These criticisms and some judicial decisions that have restricted the scope of using legislative history have not produced an actual return to the exclusionary rule. The permitted access to that history can be seen as part of a modest acceptance of a purposive approach, which represents an abandonment of a "literal rule."

When one compares England and the United States, one can perceive some movement from two powerful competing positions—that is no reliance on legislative history or heavy reliance—toward an intermediate position of some reliance, but important differences remain between the countries. In federal courts and many state courts in the United States, the use of legislative history remains more important than in England, and there is much more extensive disagreement among judges about what should be done. As already noted, the complexities of the legislative process in the United States, including the absence of a dominant party that can count on the loyalty of its representatives, makes the analysis of possible alternatives and how they are seen much harder than it is for England.

In Germany, we find some similarities and differences with both England and the United States. As in other countries, disagreements have existed about what should count as developments of legal coverage over time. The basic division has been cast as between an "objective" theory that takes the text as governing and a "subjective" theory that gives substantial weight to legislative intentions.[4] It is interesting that the subjective approach is taken as making key what was the understanding at the time of enactment, whereas the objective approach accepts that the significance of the statutory language can develop over time. These connections need not always be present. In the United States, a typical textualist takes language as meaning what it conveyed at the time of enactment, and, as in the notable case granting constitutional protection for same-sex marriage, judges may assert that the subjective intentions of enactors were to authorize development over time.

The language of Germany's Federal Constitutional Court emphasizes an objective approach in which a provision's wording and semantic content are central, but both it and the highest panels of the Federal Court of Justice do seek legislative intent by examining the history of development. As within other systems, what is put forward on the surface as the character of an approach does not actually fit all that is taken into account. Typically, such a characterization oversimplifies to a greater or lesser degree, and tends to submerge what are actual disagreements among judges about what should count and to what degree.

In Germany, as elsewhere, availability has been one argument against the use of legislative history. Of course, with all modern forms of recording and communication, actual access to what has been written in reports and spoken publicly has become much simpler, but it remains a concern in Germany that a compromise-laden process makes it hard to determine exactly how far various communications are central.[5] A constitutional argument has been made that legislative intent should be taken into account; this is an interesting contrast with the claim by some American textualists that our Constitution suggests that only enacted legislation matters.

Within Germany, what is accepted now is not a strict theory on either side. The main emphasis is on text, but evidence of legislative intent can be taken into account. Legislative history is not binding, but it can help guide what is a desirable interpretation. Statements about the aims of legislation are said to be relevant only if in some sense they are alluded to in the text. One question about legislative intentions is whether not only history leading to enactment can count, but also testimony or speeches by legislators after enactment. In the early twentieth century, the German Supreme Court accepted the relevance of such testimony, a position later rejected by the Austrian Supreme Court.[6] I am not sure whether reliance on such testimony is now precluded.[7]

In summary, we can see that within Germany, as in England and the United States, similar competing concerns are in play although the uncertainties and resolutions are a bit different.

The situation in Australia varies from both England and the United States, but the problems of clarity and an appropriate approach are not so different.[8] Australia, unlike England, has a written constitution, but that has not led courts to impose substantial restrictions on legislative choices.[9] Until fairly recently the judiciary cast its statutory interpretation in light of being a "faithful agent." However, in 2011, six of seven justices on the High Court wrote that ascertaining legislative intention amounted to "compliance with the rules of construction . . . which have been applied to reach the preferred results and which are known to parliamentary drafters and the courts."[10] Under this formulation, "intention," at least in debatable cases, becomes the result of interpretation rather than its guide.

A key rule of construction of the Court's jurisprudence is the "principle of legality," which entails that statutes are not taken to abrogate fundamental rights, unless their texts contain clear statements to that effect. The consequence is a hesitancy to construe statutes as being at odds with basic rights although that may be suggested if one looked only at the statutory language. The cases typically are cast in terms of "legislative intention," but when language is vague, judges often rely on broader principles of the legal system to determine outcomes. Some justices have seen the supposed reliance on "legislative intention" as a kind of fiction. Although the basic approach refers to interpretive standards familiar to legislators, for at least some of those standards, this familiarity is doubtful.

One way of looking at this is that when legislative provisions are vague, it is often because legislators have chosen not to resolve some basic questions—sometimes because compromise is needed for passage. For these situations we can see the Court's approach as not genuinely "interpreting" what the legislature has done, but as filling in what the legislature has left unresolved.

As with the United States and other countries, one may urge that even if their basic approaches are defensible, judges should be more honest about what is taking place and why. On the competing side is the possibility that casting matters as the objective intention of legislators may make decisions somewhat less controversial and also make producing majority decisions more easily possible for judges who differ in how much importance they give to particular factors. The issue about candor is related to the desirable complexity of actual approaches, and the extent to which judges agree on those, including the weight of various factors. These uncertainties are not limited to the United States.

What has emerged as a central question on this subject is how far actual and desirable approaches to judicial interpretation of statutes are subject to some relatively straightforward characterizations. If such approaches can be achieved in some sense, how far do they actually dictate judicial behavior, and how far is that attainable? On this question, the law of Canada provides an illuminating illustration.

In 1974 Elmer Driedger, in his book *The Construction of Statutes*, proposed a "modern rule" of statutory interpretation that applied to all cases.[11] In his second edition of 1983, he wrote, "Today there is only one principle or approach, namely, the words of an Act are to be read in their entire context and in their grammatical and ordinary sense harmoniously with the scheme of the Act, the object of the Act, and the intention of Parliament."[12] Having been mentioned in some earlier cases, that approach was adopted in 1998 by the Canadian Supreme Court in *Rizzo v. Rizzo*

Shoes Ltd.[13] The *Rizzo* case has been cited at least 92 times by the Supreme Court and more than 2,300 times by Canadian courts. Since no judicial opinions have expressed serious doubts about it, we may conclude that Canada, unlike the United States, possesses a generally accepted approach to statutory interpretation.

However, what is actually going on is much more complicated. As Ruth Sullivan, a prominent scholar who was responsible for a subsequent edition of Driedger's book, explains in an article published in 1998–1999,[14] the courts were sometimes espousing a textual approach that referred to "plain meaning" and sometimes emphasizing intentionalism. Professor Sullivan herself is sharply critical of "plain meaning" as a claimed basis for judicial decisions. She urges not only that there are various senses of meaning, such as reader understanding and writer intentions, but also different notions of plain meaning, such as "ordinary meaning, literal meaning, common sense meaning" and other possibilities.[15] As I have explained, I do think the meaning of instructions, including legal requirements, is sometimes plain in any relevant sense, but this is rarely if ever true about terms whose coverage is debated within an appellate court. Unless that term is defined more narrowly, it will not be the objective guide to resolve those debates.

One problem is how far the "co-text" is relevant. To take an example used by Sullivan, in the case of *R. v. McCraw*[16] was a man's threat to a rape a young woman forbidden by a statutory provision that made it criminal to utter a "threat to cause death or serious bodily harm to any person"? A threat of rape does concern serious physical harm, but it does not really approach a threat of death. It is arguable whether in this setting "serious bodily harm" should be read in isolation or qualified in relation to the reference to "death." The court's finding coverage chose the first option, relying on the ordinary meaning of the term. Although judges often assert "plain meaning," that not infrequently conceals what really counts in debatable cases.

When one compares Canada with the United States, it is very important to grasp the components of the formula of Elmer Driedger, which has been widely accepted. One must consider the statutory words in their "entire context" and "ordinary sense harmoniously" with the "scheme" and "object" of the Act and "the intention of Parliament." This actually allows consideration of a range of factors. Judges may well disagree about what one of these indicates and what weight it should be accorded. The consequence is that while purportedly sticking to an accepted practice of interpretation, judges will see the basic standard a bit differently, consider various factors, and be influenced by their personal outlooks. In other words, despite the presence of a dominating articulated approach, it is far from clear that the actual practices of judges within Canada vary sharply from what takes place in the United States.

We can imagine three possible conclusions about what should take place. One is that we need clear rules that will genuinely guide judges. That reformation would apply not only in the United States but also in Canada. As I have indicated in prior chapters, I do think the complexity of relevant factors and their appropriate weight makes it very hard to produce clear rules of interpretation that will resolve all, or nearly all, cases. A recommendation urged by Professor Sullivan is to explicitly adopt "pragmatism" as the right approach. That allows weight to text and intentions and broader considerations, and recognizes that we cannot expect judges to agree on the right results for difficult cases. Among other things, pragmatism can explicitly recognize that judges are not only "faithful" servants of legislators but have an independent or "supervisory" role,[17] a responsibility to avoid irrational, unjust, or unfair results even if a provision points toward that.

The third conclusion is not exactly a recommendation. If one thinks of the uncertainties and disagreements that exist within the United States about how to formulate standards of statutory interpretation, one might conclude that they are not as troubling as is often supposed. It turns out that in jurisdictions with formulated standards that are widely accepted, the realities of practice are not radically more coherent than in American courts. I am not suggesting that greater coherence and agreement are not desirable objectives, but for much of our lives, given people's differences in perspectives, these are hard to achieve, and we would do well to acknowledge that such a lack of settled standards within law that provide clear answers is not necessarily a disaster.

IV. INTERPRETING CONTRACTS

In all countries with courts, one function of judges is interpreting contracts. Some of these contracts directly involve government officials, but the vast majority is between private entities, including ordinary persons, businesses, both large and small, and other private organizations, such as hospitals and universities. For many matters, what a contract entails are straightforward: it fits the language and the intentions of those that made it. But these are not typically the situations that reach higher courts. When the crucial question is not simply how parties actually have behaved but what it is that their contract requires, we can see, as previous chapters indicate, a range of considerations that can be relevant. Most obviously, we have the simple concerns about the place of text versus intent. Should a contract be taken as its explicit language indicates, or in accord with what the parties intended? Insofar as they count, how should the text and intentions be understood? Also important is how far concerns about fairness should be given weight. These concerns can be affected not only by the actual rights and obligations a contract seems to contain, but whether any equality existed for the parties in how their contract was made, and whether one party was even likely to be aware of its terms. With advances in technology, including extensive use of electronic communication, contracts made by businesses with consumers or employees have terms the businesses have formulated, and the other parties implicitly accept them often without being even aware of many details. These developments in the frequency of particular practices can affect how courts look at things, whether or not the judges explicitly acknowledge that.

When one thinks of approaches in different countries, two dissimilarities with statutory interpretation are worth mentioning. One is that a country's political organization does not play nearly as central a role as it may for constitutional and statutory interpretation. A second dissimilarity concerns the place of the common law. In countries within that tradition, the exercise of contractual interpretation was once mainly a matter of common law developed by courts. In those countries, including the United States, we now have statutes that deal directly with aspects of this subject, either for contracts generally or specific kinds of contracts. But the role of common law, and how it should be exercised, remains. In civil law countries, we have no such tradition.

Similarities that exist in most, perhaps all, countries are what we have looked at for the United States. One is that what has been taken as appropriate interpretation has not been fixed given the passage of time and development in how society functions. The second is that we are not likely to find complete clarity and congruence between what are cast as dominant doctrines and all that judges take into account. Further, judges are not likely to be explicit and candid about everything that matters. In what follows, we shall see how many of these aspects come into play in jurisdictions outside the United States. With respect to all forms of judicial interpretation, one relevant question is what will best reflect and promote a just and healthy society. For contracts, we have not only the simple question of what is fair for people who engage in these legally enforceable agreements. Given that a great many contracts are crucial to financial relations and economic welfare, one problem is what judicial approaches will promote more general fairness and efficiency in the economic realm.

In other common law countries as well as the United States, approaches to contracts were once mainly formalist, relying on the "plain meaning" of a contract's terms. We have had a shift in England, Australia, and New Zealand, which now accept more contextual approaches and see "plain meaning" as extending beyond the literal sense of words.[18] In the United States, modern doctrine is becoming less formalist and more responsive to "concerns of morality and policy."[19] In recent years, formalism has undergone resurgence in many contract decisions, but "plain meaning" remains more contextual than it once was.

We can see the general shift away from formalism as partly related to the reality that a new technology, and the contractual relations it produces, can yield shifts both in the nature of the terms of many contracts and the degree of genuine involvement of the parties who are subject to them. In all common law jurisdictions, the text continues to play the central role for interpreting a contract, but that is typically seen now in terms of what a "reasonable person" would understand. As I have explained in earlier chapters, an actual or "reasonable" person understands a communication not solely in terms of the words but also in relation to context.

One generalization about differences between English and American law is that our rules of contract interpretation are "simpler," but it does not follow that the place of various bases for judgment or the processing of claims is actually simpler.[20] A standard such as "reasonable" invites a judgment involving many considerations; a larger collection of rules, such as England has, may be more precise.

With these general observations, I will turn to a specific issue that concerns both proper approaches and questions about conceptualization. When a court takes a contract as involving something not conveyed explicitly by the terms themselves, is that a matter of "interpretation" or judges "filling in a contractual gap"? Or is this apparent conceptual difference not real? Lord Hoffman urged in an English case that these two endeavors involve closely related analytical exercises in a system that adopts a "contextualist-objective" theory that a contract's coverage should be mainly determined by what a reasonable observer, in context, would perceive as the parties' intentions.[21] In 2015, the U.K. Supreme Court rejected this as "confusing" and "practically unhelpful,"[22] but that does not really show it as essentially misguided, since we need to know if there is a clearer, more solid alternative that will yield better decisions, or at least equally good decisions with less effort.

It may help to start on this with a brief theoretical explanation. Suppose we take "gap filling" as supplying terms that are actually omitted from the contract itself. If this is necessary, and the basis for doing so is the text of the contract and the apparent intentions of the parties, then plainly this is one aspect of interpreting the contract. Suppose instead judges fill in according to what they believe serves community values, although this is in a way at odds with the text and intentions. This would be a form of judicial independence that does not follow ordinary interpretation of the contract's content. In this simple version, as previous chapters reveal, we may find not only various degrees of involvement that are part of "interpretation," but also judicial endeavors that reach beyond that. For example, judges might decide to rely on their own evaluation even if interpretation points in the contrary direction, but only if it does so mildly rather than very strongly.

Things become more complicated if one "interprets" a contract in accord with how a reasonable observer would understand it in context. Under this standard, what finally counts are not the subjective intentions of the parties, as is the law in many civil law jurisdictions, but how what they have done would be taken by an objective observer. Such an observer might well take matters of fairness and social desirability into account. On that understanding, the filling of gaps would not be distinguishable from the forms of interpretation. A judge deciding what words to add or eliminate would be seeking the approach that a form of objective observer, who would lack any single methodology, would employ.

Within England, we have had the development of interpretive methods so that gap filling is not typically distinguishable from deciding what the contract contains. Although the observation by Lord Hoffman that no line separates these two was later rejected by the country's Supreme Court, that alone tells us neither what exactly judges will take into account, and defend as relevant, nor how far they will be moved by the same factors they use to determine the actual coverage of the contract itself, or if they do what will constitute engagement in a kind of independent evaluation. These uncertainties are closely similar to those in the United States, which has also experienced shifting doctrines whose effect on how judges actually decide is not obvious.

A particular question about the relation between interpretation and independent judgment is what judges should do about terms that are clear enough, but are unfair or unwise in some way. As mentioned earlier, this problem takes on particular importance when the terms of the contract are dictated by a large company, and consumers or others must merely accept those terms, often without even being aware of their content. In a case decided by English judges,[23] an employee who was losing his position following a bank's reorganization had signed a form that he would accept the terms set out in documents as "full and final" settlements. The bank later collapsed because of broad corruption. The House of Lords had previously indicated that employees in such a circumstance would have a claim for "stigma damages." The question was whether those who signed the release form were precluded from making such claims. Without relying directly on equitable principles, the majority in the House of Lords court ruled by a contextual interpretation that the parties would not have intended to preclude all claims of whatever nature; thus, a claim for stigma damages was not foreclosed. Although this was not acknowledged by the four judges in the majority, their conclusion was rather clearly at odds with the plain language of the signed form, although it fit with what was fair and with the wisdom of not allowing banks and others to avoid stigma damages for serious misbehavior.

This case provides an example of how judges may address elements of unfairness and inequality through interpretation rather than unconscionability. As Catherine Mitchell explains, this approach results in some lack of transparency in what counts for a "contextual" understanding.[24]

Although this example concerns the policing of a contract rather than ordinary enforcement, it does show how a "contextualist" approach can be seen in various ways that differ as to exactly what counts and how much weight various considerations may carry. According to Mitchell, scholarly literature in the United States generally assimilates contextualism with "relationalism or socio-legal approaches to contracts, as contrasted with neo-formalism."[25] Within England, contextualism is not generally taken to allow express contact terms to be overridden by trade customs and other norms external to its terms. However accurate this may be about deciding what a contract generally contains, the "stigma damages" case does show that English judges are willing to restrict or stretch ordinary language to avoid applications they regard as unjust.

One important aspect of contract interpretation that I shall not explore in any depth is the relevance of statutes that dictate practices. In common law countries, these can supplant what the common law courts have developed, and differences in statutes are one basis for various approaches. In the United States, a key provision of the federal Uniform Commercial Code recognizes the right of courts to void or reform terms that are "unconscionable." Since the code does not define this term, that leaves judges a good bit of discretion. Within England, some national statutes, such as the Consumer Credit Act and the Sale of Goods Act, function in a similar way.[26] Also important in England has been the European Union's law, which can have a significant effect on the law of all countries in the European Union. Its direct relevance for England, once it withdraws from the European Union, may be unclear, but given financial interactions, one assumes that significance will not disappear.

This provides one example of a general trend we can expect to continue to take place. As international connections become closer and closer, and more and more business dealings connect to two or more countries, the desirability increases that standards of contract interpretation, whatever their formality, fit together in practical consequences.

Just how courts should respond to what seem to be unfair formulations dictated by substantial businesses is, as we have seen, complicated in various ways. One interesting question is who should be protected here. Individual consumers and employees are obviously in that category, but what of small businesses that must go along with what a large business dictates? Many special statutory protections do not extend to them, but a plausible argument exists that they also should be recognized as often not being equal partners. English statutes do provide some protections for small businesses, but they are more limited than what applies to consumer contracts. Apparently European courts have been more encouraging for small businesses getting fair treatment, but this has not had much influence within England.[27]

Two closely related United States cases reveal how far from simple it can be to characterize the formation of a contract and whether it was fair. In cases involving the company of Gateway, two customers had each offered over the telephone to buy a computer.[28] The company shipped each product with a variety of standard terms, including an agreement to use arbitration if there was any complaint. Such arbitration terms are a common feature of such contracts, one whose status is debatable. One court accepted Gateway as having made the offer, and the consumer of having accepted it by not sending the product back within thirty days. The other court treated the original phone call as an offer that was accepted by

Gateway with proposed modifications. By not responding, the consumer had not accepted these terms. The first court ruled that the consumer was bound by the arbitration requirement; the second court said that the consumer was not.

Within the United States, "substantive unconscionability" is one way of addressing unfair terms. Often cast as whether a provision "shocks the conscience," this approach has been criticized as "absurdly subjective" and as lacking determinate content.[29]

Among the issues regarding contracts as well as other forms of interpretation is what should count as relevant evidence for what a contract covers. In many countries, including England, conduct subsequent to the formation does not count; in others, including the United States, this can be taken into account.[30] Here, I think we have a clear divide between intrinsic relevance and saving costs. How parties behave under a contract can possibly reflect how they understand its terms and what is fair, although sometimes the behavior may have other reasons. However, for judges to have to delve into and evaluate the conduct need not be simple, and may sometimes be the basis to support what is in fact a claim to avoid one's obligations. As with an emphasis on text rather than intent, there is a practicality argument to preclude such evidence.

Although in earlier times the common law of England and the United States was closely matched, the approaches are now said by Mark Gergen to be different.[31] The American approach makes it somewhat easier for courts to get into underlying issues, although this may also mean it is harder to discern what a case's outcome will be before a decision is made.

V. WILLS

I shall say very little about wills because I do not believe there are significant differences in various jurisdictions about their content and because, with a few exceptions, what is done with wills does not concern basic premises of legal systems. One exception I will not explore is when a will is set up in a way to avoid tax liabilities. Judges might be more or less accepting of terms that do that. Another exception concerns limits of what wills are allowed to do in relation to families. If someone must leave some money to a spouse or to children, the will cannot effectively provide otherwise.

A brief look at what *Theobald on Wills* has conveyed about English practices has suggested that they do not differ significantly from the United States.[32] Wills differ from each other, and prior cases do not bear significantly on how a particular will is interpreted. The will's language, of course, is key, but that includes what it reveals about purposes; and direct evidence of intentions is now often admissible, although subjective evidence of intentions typically is not.

An illustration of the kind of evidence of intentions that would be admitted is provided by the example of the testator who used the wrong middle initial of a close friend so that the name the will referred to was of a complete stranger.

In some contrast to contracts and statutes, courts cannot generally supply provisions that the will does not include, although children born after the will was written may be included.[33] An earlier chapter suggests the hypothetical of a parent who believes that a son has been killed abroad in wartime, and so leaves the same amount of money to each of the remaining children. If, shortly after the testator's death, it becomes apparent that the son had been captured and incarcerated by the enemy for some years and is now free, should the will be carried out exactly as written or should the son be given an equal share, at least absent any evidence that the parent had a negative view about him? Adding him among those who benefit definitely seems the better solution.

Words in wills are given their ordinary meaning. We looked earlier at the English case of *re Rowland* in which the court said the deaths of a couple from a ship accident in the Pacific did not "coincide" because there was no evidence that the deaths were "simultaneous." Given that judges had strong evidence that the deaths were at most minutes apart, and the genuine flexibility of the term "coincide," I urged in Chapter 1 that the decision was too rigidly literalist and was misguided. I wonder if English judges would now reach the same conclusion; although Theobald expresses no doubts about this case, he does recognize that many words and phrases may have more than one ordinary meaning.[34] He also indicates that a testator may use a sense different from ordinary meaning and have that apply if it is clear from all the provisions of the will and surrounding circumstances.[35] If they can identify an "overriding intention," judges may even supply omitted words or change words.[36] How would this apply to the hypothetical parent's omission of the son and to the meaning of "coincide" in the *Rowland* case? The omission was not a mistake in words used, but an unawareness of factual realities. This could be seen as different from a mistake within the will. In respect to "coincide," someone might say we have no convincing evidence that any meaning other than "simultaneous" was intended, but that is unpersuasive. Both situations provide strong reasons for construing the wills in accord with a testator's broad objectives, even if the language is indecisive or contrary.

When we look at this brief account of English law, which stresses how the interpretation of wills connects to contract interpretation, we can see close similarities with American law and the sorts of situations that raise questions. (I assume that things are not so different in other countries, but I have not undertaken research on that.)

VI. ADMINISTRATIVE AGENCIES AND ADMINISTRATIVE LAW

A subject explored in earlier chapters that I do not tackle here is the place of administrative agencies in relation to the law. In countries where this matters, are they seen as aspects of the executive branch or the legislative branch or some combination? For statutory laws that confer power on such agencies, how far do they have the authority to provide more precise rules about the behavior of organizations and individuals? And what range of discretion do they have when it comes to interpreting relevant statutes and their own regulations? In the United States, the somewhat controversial *Chevron* case involves a substantial deference by judges to the determinations of agencies. An exploration of the practices of other countries might reveal similarities and differences that could relate to broader variation in cultural assumptions and the role of courts. It is necessary to explore how the practices of other countries are similar and different.

VII. CONSTITUTIONAL LAW

I shall not try to cover this complex topic in great depth, but I will touch on a number of questions about other countries. These include: How far within countries with written constitutions that are sometimes applied to constrain legislation and executive action will judges use interpretive techniques similar to those in the United States? Is interpretation originalist or evolutionary? How far do the ease of amendment and the time and procedure of formulation affect how a constitution is interpreted, as contrasted with dominant political outlooks that change over modest periods of time? Are countries different enough in origins and composition so that those in one country will not have a substantial source of insight from constitutional interpretive practices in other countries? Interestingly, Justice Scalia, who was the leading source of promotion of originalism in the United States, said specifically in an opinion that "comparative analysis [is] inappropriate to the task of interpreting a constitution."[37] But that practice has occurred in many countries.[38]

I believe it helps to start with an important clarification and qualification as to what we can conclude about different countries. Techniques of constitutional interpretation are more clearly tied to political stances than other aspects of legal interpretation. When in the early twentieth century, the Supreme Court was striking down forms of economic regulation, liberals advocated for greater acceptance of legislative choices. In more modern times, with issues such as abortion and same-sex marriage, liberals have been more accepting of judicial expansion of constitutional rights. Advocates of originalism, in regard to the application of provisions, now have generally been on the politically conservative side. What this shows is that if we look at present practices of constitutional interpretation, the explanation, at least in the United States, may owe as much to contemporary political realities as basic governmental and cultural structures. To be clear, I am not asserting that Supreme Court justices will broadly try to decide cases in the way that fits their political preferences. But if justices are appointed by the president and approved by the Senate, their interpretive views are likely to fit with those that are politically dominant. A modern example of this was the republican Senate's approval of Donald Trump's appointment of Justice Neil Gorsuch, roughly a year after the Senate had avoided approving the man Barack Obama sought to appoint.

Two related factors that can bear on interpretation are when a constitution was adopted and what significance it then carried and now carries. In the United States, the basic document and important provisions included after the Civil War were adopted long ago. The basic structure involved a new country that had broken from British control; the constitution carried powerful significance. The post-Civil War amendments represented basic principles of racial equality. These periods of formulation illustrate a point made generally by Mark Tushnet that "constitutions emerge out of each nation's distinctive history and express its distinctive character."[39]

Two other countries that evolved from control by Great Britain are Canada and Australia. But in neither of them was there a sharp break.[40] It probably follows that their constitutions do not carry the same symbolic significance as in the United States. In the Union of South Africa, the constitution represents a rejection of treatment of African natives that remained unjust well into modern times.[41] Malaysia and Singapore are former British colonies that did not become independent until after the Second World War. How far does it matter if their constitutions were adopted fairly recently?[42]

The actual aspect of a constitution that seems to bear the most direct relation to what interpretive approaches make sense is the difficulty of amendments. If the process is quite difficult, that seems to provide a strong reason for interpretation that is somewhat flexible, especially when it comes to the application of open-ended provisions. One hopes that a constitution in a relatively stable liberal democracy will last for centuries. When one reflects on views about capital punishment, government regulation of economic matters, equality of women and members of different races, and the acceptability of homosexual relations, we can understand that this century has experienced a number of radical shifts since the original constitution and the post-Civil War Fourteenth Amendment. For constitutional rights to be responsive to this, we need either amendments or flexible judicial interpretation.

A number of modern countries have provisions in their constitutions that are not subject to amendment.[43] These tend to be provisions that reflect core values. In the United States, no state can be denied equal representation in the Senate without its consent; but putting this aside, every part of the federal Constitution is subject to formal amendment. In some countries, courts have declared that certain amendments have themselves actually been unconstitutional,[44] and that has occurred within some of our states according to their own constitutions,[45] but no federal amendment has been treated in this way. However, when it comes simply to how hard the amendment process is, estimated partly in terms of actual amendments, ours is one of the most difficult in the world.[46] Among the countries in which achieving amendment is much simpler are Germany and South Africa.[47]

I shall not delve into details of interpretive practices in other countries or within individual states within the United States. But I shall mention some variations. For some of these practices, we may be able to understand why what is done in various countries differs; for others, we have no simple explanations. In Germany, the Constitutional Court has tended to give less importance to framers' intent than has been true throughout much of U.S. history (although this reliance is now controversial here).[48] The German Court has more directly relied on modern values than has been common for the U.S. Supreme Court, although that played a critical role in the *Obergefell v. Hodges* decision creating a constitutional right for same-sex marriage. In Australia, in which the constitution was actually enacted as an imperial statute, the High Court has been dominantly textualist, treating the constitution essentially like statutes,[49] although acknowledging that it is special and needs a somewhat flexible approach for changing circumstances.[50] The Constitutional Court of South Africa, in contrast to the country's earlier history in which those who controlled society embraced the fundamental injustice of apartheid, has in modern times engaged in a transformative process in which it seeks to ensure a just recognition of fundamental rights.[51] The Canadian Supreme Court has adopted an interpretive approach that is largely purposive.[52]

One basic approach to constitutional interpretation is originalism; its role in the United States is contested. The fundamental idea is that original understanding should be key. As we have seen, this alone does not tell us about the respective role of framers' intent in comparison with reader understanding, and it also does not tell us to what degree original understanding of interpretation itself matters, a subject that played a prominent role in Justice Kennedy's majority opinion in the *Obergefell* case. We should briefly look at some various views about originalism in other countries. In an article showing that originalism is not limited to the United States, Yvonne Tew explores its use in the relatively new contexts of Malayasia and Singapore.[53] In Malaysia, in which the role of the dominant Islamic religion is a major issue, original understanding has been tied by judges to expansive constitutional interpretation.[54] Rather than focusing on what the text would have meant objectively at the time of formation, the judges give more attention to the historical background at the time the constitution was drafted.[55] In contrast, the Supreme Court of Singapore, influenced by the British tradition of parliamentary supremacy, has typically employed a strict legalism that takes a literalist approach to the constitutional text.[56]

These illustrations, as well as a study of different "originalist" approaches in the United States, show how even when it comes to this broad approach, we have no clear strategy of interpretation. What exactly is going on will depend on cultural background, government organization including the perceived roles of judges, and political positions. When we look at different countries and how various judges interpret and apply their constitutional provisions, we can understand that certain factors, such as the age and symbolic importance of the constitution, and the ease or difficulty of amendment, are likely to affect interpretive approaches, but we have no simple correlation that if "factor A" is present, the interpretation strategy will be strict originalism or a particular alternative.

A still broader lesson is one reflected by a wide range of subjects in this book. However straightforward an announced technique of interpretation may be, when it comes to resolving genuinely difficult cases, judges on the highest courts are likely to take multiple factors into account. These may or may not be well reflected in their opinions, but, even if they are, it is very hard for outsiders to accurately assess the comparative weight of various considerations. This is not simply a "problem" of American constitutional law. It is a consequence of the complexity of human life and the formation and application of standards of behavior.

5

Other Disciplines

Insights and Limits

I. INTRODUCTION

In this chapter, I examine other disciplines and what their concepts of interpretation may convey about what takes place and what should take place within the law. We can conceive of various connections. For example, it is possible that an approach from another discipline has a direct application for how judges should understand legal provisions. More modestly, understanding how interpretation takes place in other disciplines might provide an insight into legal interpretation, without a definitive answer as to how such interpretation should take place. Other disciplines also provide insight into how the law differs, and why judicial action should not be the same as the practices in one or more other domains. A final kind of relation exists when the insights or claims within another discipline are directly relevant for the content of the law. For example, how people generally understand one another might impact how the content of a contract between two people should be understood.

One lesson of this inquiry is that law is not the only area for which we have no simple answer as to how practically people do and should interpret, and as to how we should conceptualize such interpretation. The complexities of interpretation and conceptualization are neither limited to law nor a clear indication of flawed practice.

I should note that my overall thesis here fits with the preceding chapters. I do not believe that either theories about particular areas of our social life or general theories of interpretation can answer the hard questions about how judges and other officials should understand the law. In essence, difficult questions remain, and can be addressed primarily by focusing on our system of government and the roles of officials within it. Theories beyond the law provide only limited guidance about debatable cases.

We can distinguish between theories about interpretation in other distinct areas and more general theories that claim a broader coverage. Among the more particular areas are religious interpretation, literary and critical interpretation, performance of plays and music, and informal communication. Two broader approaches are the philosophy of language and general theories of interpretation that cover all domains. The chapter begins with religious interpretation and other particular domains, then turns to general theories, and finishes with informal communications and instructions. This ordering reflects my general thesis that, to a large extent, it is such instructions that give us the closest analogy as to how the law should be understood.

I should at the outset make clear a decided limitation of this chapter. Many of the leading theories in these other areas are themselves rich and complex. I do not attempt to explain and analyze them in detail, something that would require thousands of pages. My aim is to provide readers a basic sense of what these claims amount to and to explain briefly how far these claims plausibly relate to how judges interpret in various domains of the law.

II. RELIGIOUS INTERPRETATION

I shall begin with religious interpretation. A reader may find this peculiar since in our liberal democracy, which contains a "no establishment" clause in the First Amendment and is now largely secular, at least politically, we definitely do not expect judges to explicitly rely on religious bases when they interpret contracts and statutes. Of course, if judges are interpreting a contract that is directly about responsibilities within a religious denomination, they may need to give attention to the understandings of that body.

The reasons to start here are a bit different. One aspect of any religion is that it contains specific or general principles, or both, about how we are called upon to behave. Since the law concerns how people should act toward one another, religious interpretation is more closely analogous to law than something like literary interpretation.[1]

For much of human history, claims about the proper ways to construe authoritative writing concentrated on the Bible and other religious texts. Questions included how to construe provisions whose literal understanding or application had come to seem dubious. Two obvious examples are how we should understand all the miracles noted in biblical passages, and certain specific indications of how we should treat others and ourselves. Should we, for example, always "turn the other cheek" if someone attacks and injures us? A crucial question in all this is how we should understand indicated relations of men and women and negative references to homosexual involvement. Interestingly, during early Christian times, certain "gospels" afforded women greater equality than passages in what became the New Testament;[2] nevertheless, the main questions about interpretation have concerned how the Bible should be taken, not how to interpret these largely forgotten writings that did not get included. Should the passages be accepted as literally as possible, according to likely facts at the time, or should they be taken in an evolutionary way to fit with developing values?

Of course, a crucial feature of most religious interpretation is that it is seen as connected to what God has created on earth and how God wishes us to behave. A believer's perception about the basic relation of God to human beings is almost certainly influenced by what he takes as authoritative passages, but that core perception can also affect how he perceives those passages. Individual religious belief is not ostensibly a relevant factor for legal interpretation within our system, although personal religious convictions, whether positive or negative, can affect how people see things, a reality that can be true for interpreting judges as well as ordinary citizens. When I say this can be true, I mean to include both individuals self-consciously taking their religious beliefs into account, and people influenced by their beliefs even when they try to discount them, or are unaware their religious beliefs are playing a role.

It is worth noting at the outset two features of religious interpretation that can bear on legal interpretation, especially that of the Constitution. The first is that religious leaders and others are called upon to construe texts that were adopted long ago. They need to consider how far shifting, hopefully developing, values should be taken into account. The second feature is that within our own society, development of cultural values has been significantly influenced by changes in religious outlooks, and vice versa. If we understand how perceptions of core religious documents have developed over time, this may help us to grasp what "nonestablishment of religion" should now amount to and how far women and gay couples should be given equal rights under the equal protection clause. This, of course, would be only one small element of what might bear on a proper legal interpretation, but it does suggest that an understanding of approaches to religious interpretation is not totally irrelevant.

Another aspect of religious interpretation that can resemble legal interpretation is how much weight to give to prior understanding of passages by those in authority. On this point, different religions have contrasting traditions.

When we think about the relation between religious interpretation and that for the general law of society, we have a crucial distinction. In modern liberal democracies, the assumption is that judges and legislators should not rely directly on what they believe is right from a religious point of view. But in much of human history, and in some modern segments of the world, a broad assumption has been that the aim of the political order is to carry out what the true religion calls for. In such a society, which would include the original Mormon settlement in Utah, evaluations of what is the right religious perception could bear directly on what laws legislators believed they should adopt and on how judges and other officials should construe laws that are vague and unclear. In these situations, religious and general legal interpretation would be directly intermingled. In other settings, any relevant connection is obviously less straightforward.

With these general observations, I shall turn to more specific outlooks of religious interpretation, how they differ, and how they may tell us something about legal interpretation in our system.

The Hebrew Bible and Muslim Quran both contain much material that reflects what the law is like; the Christian New Testament has very little specification of behavior that resembles legal constraints. In Judaism, Christianity, and Islam, the interpretation of sacred texts is important, although not the only source of insight regarding what we need to believe and how we should behave. Between these religions, and within them, there are significant differences in how the central texts are now to be understood and how much importance the texts themselves carry.

I shall begin with Judaism. For Jews, the Hebrew Bible, including the Torah, believed to be given by God to Moses, and the rulings and analysis contained in the Talmud, have special authority.[3] As is also the case for Islam, the key documents are much more legalistic than is true for Christianity and the New Testament. The documents Judaism takes as authoritative have been interpreted over the centuries. As with those in secular legal systems, interpreters have needed to draw on some combination of "text, tradition, and reason." Without trying to explore just how various techniques have been used by those interpreting Jewish law for centuries, I shall mention that the intentions of the writers have not been taken as key, since the crucial passages have been seen as divinely conveyed. At least some Jews, the Orthodox, do accept certain indicated restraints as binding, notably the idea that one should not perform any work on the Sabbath. There has, however, been some developed specification as to what counts as work. The same is true about the requirement to eat kosher food. A passage in the Torah forbids cooking a kid in its mother's milk; this was extended by the Talmud to include any eating of meat with milk.

Not all passages are taken literally. The text of Deuteronomy indicates that a betrothed girl sexually taken by force in the open country is innocent, but one taken by force in the city is not. This passage has been taken as effectively making it critical whether anyone would be available to save a girl if she cries out,[4] the notion being that if she fails to do so when she could get help, she is not really innocent.

Among the most important questions about interpretation of religious texts are the significance of purposes and reasons, and the place of narratives. Narratives of events play much less of a role for ordinary legal interpretation, but here they are seen to reflect God's deep involvement. A troubling question about purposes and reasons is what to do if not only one specific provision, but a broader assumption is at odds with modern values. For example, it is hard to reconcile the biblical text and the Torah with the idea that men and women should be treated equally in most respects and that same-sex relationships should be accepted. These kinds of tensions constitute one reason many people have departed from Orthodox Judaism in favor of a more flexible understanding of their religion.

When we turn to Islam, it is noteworthy that the Muslim culture has often been characterized as a legal one. Roughly 500 pages of the central Quran have legal content. Over time, four sources of Islamic law were accepted: the Quran; the Sunna, which contains reports of the prophet Muhammad; consensus of opinion; and legal arguments including analogy.[5] To what degree Islamic law should rely on other sources such as customs of the time has been a subject of disagreement. Such disagreement has also existed about the place of reason and purpose in interpreting Islamic laws. How to regard notions of gender inequality, such as a recommended allocation to daughters of one-half the inheritance of sons, and the approval of polygamy in which a man can have multiple wives, are difficult questions that have led to disagreements about what a society's governing law should now provide and how people should exercise the liberties they have.

In brief, we can see that many disagreements over how crucial religious texts should now be understood resemble those concerning aspects of secular law. This is especially true for long-standing constitutions, but, given the basic difference between secular law and interpretation regarding what believers take as reflecting the will of God, we cannot draw any simple conclusions from one domain to the other.

I shall now turn to Christianity, which is both significantly different in respects from standard Judaism and Islam, and contains within itself a crucial division. Although Christians have supposed that the Bible establishes some norms of behavior, Christian interpretation of biblical sources concentrates much less on the meaning of law-like rules. In respect to aspects of the Hebrew Bible, the gospel of Paul treats many rules with an allegorical construction, and urges that those with faith in Christ are not bound by Jewish law. In his writing, once Christianity was established, Augustine urged that how someone interpreted particular passages was not crucial as long as he or she did not depart from God's basic messages.[6] Church fathers generally believed that scriptural interpretation needed to go beyond literal meaning.

The Catholic Church over the centuries has developed a detailed canon law, based partly on biblical passages. This law, of course, covers not only spiritual feelings, but also how people should behave in respect to matters such as abortion, sex outside of marriage, and divorce.

This canon law reflects a crucial difference between Roman Catholicism and most Protestant denominations, one that also exists among some other religions. From the beginning, the organized Christian group that became the Roman Catholic Church assigned high authority to those in leading positions. In contrast to the Gnostic Gospels, ordinary believers were supposed to accept what those in positions of leadership asserted. That remains true, as strongly reflected by the authority of the pope and cardinals. The authority of leaders carries force not only in the present. Those who provided interpretation and influence centuries ago are still taken to have a strong effect on what is now taken as true and sound. In contrast, Martin Luther and other Protestant leaders emphasized individual believers approaching the scriptures on their own, receiving inspiration from that endeavor. What was seen as the key to salvation was faith in Christ, not one's particular behavior.

The division over the role of authorities for religious belief and practices tells us nothing helpful about secular law. For that, officials must decide what is required of people and what rights they have. In practical terms, the decisions by officials with given authority are bound to be central. Of course, within a religion, the same will be true for decisions such as when to meet for worship services, unless that is put up for a general vote. But in terms of what to believe and how to practice those beliefs outside of group gatherings, a religion can function even if these are left to individual choice, not only in terms of possible enforcement but also in respect to how individuals should perceive their responsibilities. What is perceived as the appropriate influence of religious leaders differs among Jews and Muslims as well as Christians.

Of course, individuals do with some frequency interpret secular legal standards without relying directly on what judges or others have said. One sense of this is quite simple. Those who engage in contractual relations need to grasp their rights and duties prior to official involvement, and, most frequently, mutual understanding or agreed upon concessions render that involvement unnecessary. Another sense is a bit different. Individuals may have independent views about what the Constitution entails that are not dependent on authoritative decisions. Thus, a critic of *Obergefell v. Hodges* might say, "The Supreme Court made a mistake—the Constitution does not really confer a right to same-sex marriage." Such an individual view does not directly carry much practical significance, but in combination such outlooks can make a difference. If a court is aware that the vast majority of people have a particular view, judges may be hesitant to render a decision to the contrary. And, if such objections to an actual decision exist among a significant part of the population, this may affect whether effective qualifications are made to the practical import of the ruling, and increase the possibility that the ruling will be later overturned. Both these realities are present with the right to abortion granted in *Roe v. Wade*, although I believe the actual overruling is much less likely than some of those opposed to abortions may suppose.

In the last two centuries, various historical studies and modern science have led some to skepticism about the truth of various things the Bible contains, such as numerous miracles, including Mary becoming pregnant with the fetus of Jesus without sexual intercourse. This skepticism about various miracles can lead to outright disbelief or a de-emphasis on what the biblical text contains. When one looks at Christianity and other religions over time, one sees an evolution over how central documents should be perceived and what we should take as crucial guides. In this respect, religion presents an example of evolutionary interpretation that is also crucial for aspects of a secular system such as open-ended constitutional provisions. Exactly what weight should be given to past interpretations is definitely less straightforward for constitutional subjects than the clear division between Martin Luther and the Catholic tradition. However, for some subjects, such as the place and roles of women in relation to men, developments within religions that downplay the modern force of some biblical passages bear resemblance to deviations within our basic constitutional approach from reliance on historical understanding at the time the equal protection clause was passed.

This brief summary of practices of religious interpretation reveals that various questions on which legal theorists concentrate, such as the relevance of specific language compared to overall purposes and how to treat ideas that no longer correlate with the basic values of a culture, are not restricted to the domain of ordinary law. But we can also identify critical differences, such as the range of crucial considerations and whether one thinks that religious texts and interpretations are divinely inspired. Ordinary legal norms generally are to be taken literally, but that may or may not be true about various religious texts. I have mentioned that religions have different views about exactly how much weight should be assigned to interpretations by those with authority. Those disagreements tell us very little about secular legal systems. To a large extent, the roles of judges and other officials are not disputed, though it is contested just how far judges should rely on independent judgments about what the law *should* do. For these debatable questions, religious interpretation and practices are quite different, and they provide virtually no guidance for what makes sense within the legal system.

With these observations, we will turn to other kinds of interpretation.

III. LITERARY INTERPRETATION AND PERFORMANCE ACTS

We shall now look at literary interpretation and the way to perform dramatic and musical acts on stage. Each of these bears some resemblance to legal interpretation and yet differs in crucial ways. Explicit or implicit instructions about how to perform are about what people should do; literary interpretation concerns how people do and should understand written texts although that does not directly concern what they should do with the actions of their own lives. I shall begin with literary interpretation, which in modern times has actually received more theoretical concentration than religion interpretation. Again, I shall not delve into details about various sophisticated accounts; rather I shall emphasize similarities and differences with legal interpretation.

How should literary texts be interpreted, and does such interpretation yield broader insights about language, communication, and culture? What exactly constitutes "literature" is, as with many significant categories, hard to say.[7] The obvious coverage is fiction and poetry, but the term can also apply to excellent writing of history or an autobiography, or even to legal opinions and formulated legal standards that have excellent literary quality, such as the Declaration of Independence. Without claiming that we have a clear categorical division, I shall concentrate on the core of what is taken as literature, that is, fictional and poetic writing. One suggestion, made by Ronald Dworkin, is that interpretation of these is constructive or creative, as is legal interpretation, and differs from conversational interpretation, which is an ordinary attempt to understand what a speaker is saying.[8] We can see typical literary works as essentially performative, created by authors so that new stories or patterns of words will have an effect on readers.

One aspect of literary interpretation, for which we have a legal analogy, is that what counts is how we understand the author's intent. This was once a dominant approach, but it has fallen out in modern times. On that view, what constitutes the "meaning" is what the author intended. Some of the difficulties with this approach resemble those concerning the law. Given the changing meanings of some words, such as "sentimental," and of cultural assumptions, discerning the subjective intent of an author of two centuries ago can be extremely hard. Indeed, given the varying ways individuals see things and use words, it can even be difficult to discern the intent of modern authors. We need also to recognize that authors may have multiple levels of intent, and that "meaning" may need to be distinguished from the application of words and from their deeper significance. If a man says "My dog is a male," the basic meaning is straightforward; but do his tone of voice, facial expressions, and the context convey that he takes this meaning as a reinforcing of his own masculinity? This may be "significance" that a listener can or cannot grasp easily.

Even if one thinks that the "meaning" of poetry and fiction is determined by author's intent, it is hard to conclude that this controls "significance." We have two basic reasons, one of which applies to legal interpretation. The first is that as time passes, and people see things differently, it is awkward, perhaps nearly incoherent, to say that the modern "significance" of what has been written depends solely on the author's intentions. The second reason relates to how we read literature. We concentrate on what it says to us. We may have some interest in the setting of the original writing, but we do not concentrate on whether what we take as the various messages are exactly what the author intended. Different readers may well perceive the significance of a novel or a poem somewhat differently, but that is not a problem, since there is no need for a uniform grasp. In respect to assessing significance, the function of interpreting judges is quite different. They seek an approach that they believe will be, or should be, embraced by other judges.

Many of the problems concerning the passage of time, various levels of understanding, and the difficulty of discerning an author's intent apply to "meaning" as well as "significance." This can sometimes be hard for wills, contracts, and statutes, but in most of these situations we typically have some fairly straightforward direction. Given the much greater complexity within many novels and poems, it is often a lot harder to single out a particular meaning within various specific passages. One thing that is notable about "meaning" is that the author of a poem may both conceive a certain meaning as he writes, but also intend to encourage readers to supply their own meanings. In that event, one aspect of an author's total meaning would be that readers not be controlled by his more specific original meaning.

An alternative approach to author intention, one that has become much more favored for literary interpretation, is reader response.[9] On this theory for literary works, there is no single meaning since readers will respond differently. Although a reader may bring some aspect of her life experience with her when she reads anything—a reader can grasp a "No parking" sign regardless of her particular background and outlook—poems and novels are typically written so that the reader's personal outlook will affect just how she perceives them. Of course, novels often have some points and messages that are obvious, and not all legal standards are read the same way by everyone, but almost all legal standards are formulated so that there will be a dominant understanding covering most situations. A shared understanding is not needed for literature for which various understandings pose no practical problem.

A third basic approach is that what counts for "meaning" and for "significance" is what really is the best answer that could be arrived at. Since for literature, it is fine if readers disagree in their understandings, and it may be very hard to reach agreement on how one decides what is the best understanding, this approach is far from simple. It may, however, be reasonable to say that a critic who will write or speak to a general audience may seek what seems to him to be the best understanding. A critic could, however, conclude that various approaches may be best in different senses. One understanding may be the most successful artistically, one the most realistic, and yet another may convey the strongest moral message.

What can literary interpretation tell us about legal interpretation? When one seeks to understand a novel, one needs to go beyond literalism. As we have seen, this is also sometimes true for construing much of the Constitution and some statutory provisions, but there are huge differences. For many applications of law, a literal understanding is exactly what is needed, and the reasons for going beyond literalism in legal domains are different enough from literature so that in this respect a relevant grasp of literary interpretation tells us almost nothing about what interpreting judges and other officials should do.

More importantly, in regard to a relation of practical significance, novels and poems, as well as biographies and autobiographies, can teach us about human beings and our societies. Some of that writing concerns how the law itself operates, but more broadly understanding what people are like can be intrinsically relevant for making and construing aspects of law. According to one analyst, a novel of Charles Dickens shows why a rigid utilitarian approach to life does not make sense.[10] Such an insight might be relevant for a judge in some respect. More generally, since people, including judges, tend to formulate their personal perspectives in respect to their family life and close associations, reading valuable novels may broaden their understandings of a wider range of the human race in our society and in the world. Another lesson suggested about some literature is that it teaches readers to withhold judgment until they are prepared to make a finding that is more profound.

When we put all this together, we can conclude that reading and interpreting literature can provide some insight for understanding the law and what it should be. We can also identify some overlap in how the two interpretations take place. But we can easily see two huge variations. The first difference: literature is created to entertain people and promote a deeper understanding of human life and its complexities. The law tells people what they should do and what rights they have. The second difference is that when the content of law is in question, we need a decisive answer that will apply to those who litigate and will usually have a broader relevance. However hard it may be to arrive at a correct answer, judges must dictate one answer over any competitors. This is not true with respect to literature. One could see competing interpretations as having some accuracy, and even if a direct conflict exists between two of them, it is fine if some people find one persuasive and some are convinced by the other. Indeed, if one goes into all the nuances of understanding, it may be that no two people see the messages of a novel as exactly the same. Looking at the law, one could respond that no two judges facing debatable issues will have precisely the same approaches to what counts and to what degree, but the majority of judges on a court do have to reach a definite outcome. Where literature is concerned, a critic may express his perception, and ordinary readers may convey theirs to acquaintances, but there is no problem if these differ. Given that judges do need to reach agreements, giving some weight to how their colleagues interpret can be important, and outsiders like myself offering suggestions need to take into account what is feasible and plausible for judges in general. None of this is critical for someone who interprets a novel internally or explicitly.

All this tells us that the differences between literary and legal interpretation are so great that an understanding of the first will tell us almost nothing about how the debatable practical issues concerning legal interpretation should be treated.

How, if at all, are things different for music and other performing arts? We can see the writing of a musical score as a kind of law-like command about what to play, and judges are, in effect, performers of standards that have been set. In this sense, performance seems much more analogous to legal interpretation than does reading literature. One *might* think that proper performance is controlled by the intentions of the composer and see this as quite like reading a contract or a statute.

What is a performer to do if she thinks some deviation will make a piece better or will fit more with her capacities? She might believe, for example, that as time has passed and culture has changed, people would now be moved more if a piano sonata is played more quickly than the composer comprehended. Another variation concerns musical instruments themselves: Should people use modern instruments or, insofar as possible, stick with ones that duplicate those used at the time of composition?

I believe the answers here are fairly simple. At least if a piece, such as a Mozart concerto, has lasting significance, there will be numerous performances and recordings, and typically, we ordinary people can hear more than one. We may welcome hearing versions that are played on modern instruments *and* also ones like those played in Mozart's time. We may also welcome variations based on the special skills of individual performers. Although an individual or group performing is not quite the same as readers engaging in literary interpretation, since many performances may take place, particular directors and performers do not need to aim exactly for what they perceive as best for everyone else. Judges, on the other hand, do need to strive for the interpretation that is really best, at least taking into account the perspectives of fellow judges.

For this reason, thoughts about how people should decide to engage in a specific performance do not tell us a great deal about legal interpretation.

In literary interpretation and musical performance, there are two fundamental questions that relate to judicial interpretation. Should a reader or performer concentrate on discovering what was previously created, or engage at least partly in providing a creative input? Relatedly, how far is "meaning" or desirable performance determined by the writer of the text? Thoughts about these other areas can suggest interesting analogies with respect to the law, but what is needed is so different that these analogies can hardly tell us much about how legal interpretation should take place.

IV. PHILOSOPHY OF LANGUAGE AND GENERAL THEORIES OF INTERPRETATION

A different kind of possible source of insight into legal interpretation is the philosophy of language, which consists of general theories about language and its use. What can such theories tell us about what does and should take place concerning the law? I shall address here three related subjects: the nature of linguistic and other human communications, standards of linguistic meaning and the pragmatics of communication, and philosophic writing about vagueness. It is worth noting that we can easily refer to "speaker's meaning," and "sentence meaning," or "reader's meaning" without assuming they are always the same. What matters is what is most important, the key meaning for a practical choice.

On the subject of to what degree the intent of a writer or speaker is central, Paul Grice claimed for many years that intent was the key.[11] He recognized that what speakers meant did not always conform with the meaning of their sentences, and that what mattered often was a combination of natural and nonnatural meaning. What counted was what the speaker sought to convey to listeners. The analysis of Grice and his critics was very complex, but we can imagine some communications that seem to mean one thing, but lack the intent that it be taken that way. For example, a sergeant might issue an "order" that those under him shine their shoes, but he and his subordinates know that he does not want or expect the order to be carried out. Rather, he is simply satisfying a superior officer by issuing the order. Here, the meaning of the language of the order itself differs from the speaker's intent. The same is true about some formal legal constraints, calling for actions no one expects to take place.

An approach that differs from reliance on intentions is that the key to meaning is how the language used would be generally understood according to conventional understanding. This places much greater emphasis on a reader's understanding of what has been conveyed. A problem here is that not all expressions are simple and straightforward. Two people who say the same thing may mean to convey things slightly differently, and their audiences may be aware of what they are trying to do. If a man and a woman are approaching a door and she says "Treat me with respect," she might be implying that he should, or should not, hold open the door for her. When I was much younger, it was assumed that men held the doors open in general for women, but now such a gesture may seem in tension with equality. If the words, taken conventionally, are unrevealing here, the man may nevertheless grasp what the woman means if he knows her fairly well. When a woman says "Treat me with respect" in a broader context, that may place upon the listener the complex question of what various aspects she understands as "respect." A conventional account also runs into the problem of how to take instances in which someone has misspoken, using words that the listener realizes do not fit his intended meaning. If I tell students to show up at 3:00 a.m., is the conventional account of meaning the actual time of 3:00 a.m., or does it include what would be a plausible time for students to meet faculty, that is, 3:00 p.m.?

Whether for ordinary communication, speaker intent or conventional meaning is somehow central does not really help resolve difficult legal questions. Given the death of a will writer, and the reasons not to rely on the testimony of competitors for assets, one might think conventional meaning should govern, but what if there is clear, undisputed evidence that the writer meant something different? We have looked at the striking example when the testator used the wrong middle initial for the Robert Krause he knew well.[12] For contracts, a reason to rely on conventional understanding may be that it is usually too hard to discern if parties had competing senses.

What should a court have done if it concluded that a statute requiring that claims be made "before December 31" was really aimed at the end of the year, and legislators did not mean to exclude claims made on December 31? A more troubling question is when the simple understanding of statutory language does not fit with some fundamental purpose or value. Was the Supreme Court right in the *Holy Trinity Church* case[13] not to preclude a contract with a foreign minister to enter the country though that was covered by the basic statutory language and was not included in named exemptions?

When it comes to how the Constitution should be interpreted, general observations about meaning have much less relevance. As we have seen, some central constitutional provisions and even some precedents interpreting them are characterized by vagueness and indeterminacy.

An issue on which philosophers have disagreed is whether there is a correct answer to every question of possible fit of a concept. The reality is that sometimes but not always we have a definite answer. When a person is "bald" is a bit vague at the edges. Although most people are not bald and some, including myself, are, it is impossible to say on which day exactly a person crosses the line. Indeed, whether someone counts as bald may well depend on why it matters, if it does. If someone is in the middle of becoming arguably bald, perhaps he should not count as "bald" if the law requires bald people to wear hats, but he should benefit if a law grants money to pay for treatments of bald people to grow hair. About some other vague terms, one may think that in general there is a correct answer about all possible applications, however hard it may be to discern what they are. This could be true for an elderly person deciding what is the most "just distribution" of her assets. She may be fully aware that it is nearly inconceivable she will perceive the best answer, but she may still believe such an answer exists. This is similar to the faith of many religious people that there is a best answer as to how they should live, however far removed this may be from what they can ascertain.

The basic questions about vagueness connect to whether one sees judges as interpreting and applying law, or as making law, when they reach conclusions about the coverage of vague concepts. Although judges' own perceptions about whether the law contains a correct answer, however complex that determination may be, can affect what they take into account and what weight they accord various factors, across the board no straightforward application is present.

What can we conclude from all this? Philosophical writings on vagueness and indeterminacy may well help to reveal the problems that face judges in some cases, especially those dealing with broadly cast individual rights. These philosophical writings may also suggest why if a judge is persuaded by one outlook or another, that could affect how exactly she sees her responsibility in such cases. But we have no clear, simple connection between the philosophical insights and the disagreements over how actual judges do and should perceive things and see their responsibilities. This is partly because a crucial question is how much other parts of the law bear on how vague provisions should be treated. The general difference between writer intentions and conventional meaning can also be illuminating, but no general observations about ordinary communications can tell us just how judges should understand matters, especially given the special status of law and the limits on how far judges are able to discern factual truths.

A somewhat different general approach is one that focuses on "interpretation" but develops a broad theory that applies to how it takes place in the wide range of human attempts to understand. Modern theories of this sort have reached beyond texts to a wide variety of social practices and events.[14] Among the crucial considerations are the relations of a text to an interpreter, and the fact that a historical and social context often renders it difficult or impossible for readers to recapture the original understanding of writers. For law as well as many other disciplines, an important issue is whether a particular interpretation can be objectively right or wrong. I have suggested that for literary interpretation, this is actually much less central. Does interpretation of various writings improve or worsen, or simply vary as time passes, and different people make the effort?

I shall give some attention to the notable theory of Hans-Georg Gadamer without exploring it in-depth.[15] He urged that present interests motivate interpretation and that it involves "historically effected consciousness." Tradition is a part of us; with a nameless authority, it significantly determines "our intentions and attitudes." Gadamer conceived interpretation as a kind of dialogue between the text and the interpreter. To provide a personal illustration, I once read Clifford Geertz's essay on Balinese cockfighting,[16] which claimed that betting large amounts of money represented a kind of emotional investment in the outcome. As one who had played sports in high school and college and rooted strongly for some professional teams, I was initially dubious about that assertion, but as I reflected I acknowledged both that cultures can matter here and that my own attitudes may well have been more personal and less "natural" than I had supposed. My pre-understanding affected my reading, but the reading enriched my understanding.

In Gadamer's account, "interpretation" includes simple understanding and application as well as what the narrower use of the term is taken to cover. When he considers "orders," he says that a failure to carry them out is not always "disobedience," because the recipient must reach beyond the mind of the person giving the order, but also consider the situation and what would be responsible action.

As with many legal theorists who focus on Supreme Court cases, Gadamer underemphasizes those situations in which there is a clear meaning to what has been said that will be grasped by those receiving the communication. To take examples of a descriptive statement and a kind of instruction: "It is now 48 degrees Fahrenheit out and will rise to 55 degrees this afternoon"; "Please pass the salt." These communications will be understood in the same way by different people even if the influence on their lives varies. The area of law to which Gadamer's general theory has the most obvious relevance is the Constitution with its long-standing open-ended provisions that need to be construed in modern times. Present outlooks and a developing culture affect how long-standing standards are now understood for application.

General theories of interpretation, like specific explanations of other disciplines, can reveal aspects of what is likely and what is wise in legal interpretation. Notably they can tell us that recapturing original understanding decades or centuries later is very difficult and usually impossible, and they can also provide broad reasons why it is healthy to interpret in light of what matters to those now engaging in that exercise. But general theories cannot tell us exactly what does and should matter in forms of legal interpretation and how much different elements should count. The law is special in its creation of formal requirements, with fair notice important for many of these, and with final decisions rendered by judges who need to seek an interpretation persuasive to other judges. The general theories can tell us something about what it would be unrealistic to expect and propose, but given vast variations in the kinds of communications that require us to interpret, and huge differences in the fundamental objectives of interpretation, we cannot suppose that a theory that reaches all these forms will provide decisive practical answers to what is and what should be taking place with debatable topics of legal interpretation.

V. INFORMAL INSTRUCTIONS

As I have illustrated in other chapters and noted at the start of this one, the use of language most like that in the law involves informal instructions that tell people what to do. Although the formal requirements of law differ, when we reflect on other instructions we can grasp much of what is involved in interpreting law and why we have no simple contextual answers as to how exactly that should take place.

I shall begin with three examples and then explore some of the nuances about meaning and performance. A parent who must be away for a week gives a hired babysitter instructions about where to shop and what food to buy for her children. A basketball coach, with his team on the offense and ahead by three points with only twenty seconds left, tells his players, "Don't take any shots." A professor tells his students to show up at 3:00 a.m., a clear mistake.

What do the coach's and professor's instructions "mean"? Assuming that the professor made a kind of error, literal meaning here does not fit clear intentions. What is uncertain about the coach is whether he really wants his players to refrain from taking extremely easy shots that they almost always make and that would add two points to assure a victory. We could ascribe a "meaning" according to an instructor's literal language, to general usage of that sort, to the speaker's intentions, to his understanding of what he said, or to the understanding of a reasonable or highly perceptive listener. If we ask what is *the* meaning, the answer is that we can have different senses of "meaning" according to our ordinary uses of that term. When the law settles on one of these as what counts as "the meaning" for a particular provision, that is because we need a definite answer as to what the law requires. But these illustrations help to show why a general analysis of what communications "mean" when speaker intent differs from listener understanding will not itself answer the question of what judges should take as most important.

I should note here that even when one person is making the assessment, the context may be important. Suppose during the time out, a tall player asks the coach, "What should I do if I have a chance to dunk the ball into the basket?" The coach might respond, "What I said means don't take any shot unless it is extremely easy. A dunk is not covered." Suppose, instead, no one raises the question and a player with an opportunity declines to take a very easy shot. After the game another player says to the coach, "You should really criticize him for hurting the team's chance to win." The coach might respond, "I can't do that. He was following what I had told you all to do."

It is generally fair to say that those instructed will usually take what is said in accord with what they consider the speaker's intentions, but even here we have two qualifications, one of which is subtle. The first is when an instruction is given to a group that does not have the ability to probe into intentions or discuss what should be done. Imagine that the coach tells his players to carry out a play with a certain title. One player is virtually certain the coach really meant a play with a slightly different title, but if others are going along with the literal instruction, he will need to do so too. A more subtle example can be attached to the "Don't take any shots" instruction. Suppose a player says to himself, "I don't think our coach meant to preclude this easy shot but I'm not sure. If I take the shot against his wishes, he may be quite angry. On the other hand if I refrain, he can't really blame me for doing what he said." In the latter instance, the coach may blame himself, not the player, for the mistake. Put more generally, if those subject to an instruction are uncertain about the speaker's intentions, they may have a reason to follow literal terms even if they believe those terms probably do not reflect the intentions. In those circumstances, it is hard to say that either the player who shoots, or the one who doesn't, has failed to comply with what the coach has said. Saying what counts as "faithful performance" in that setting is not simple. Does concern about a possible, but less probable than not, reaction by the coach count?

Matters become more complicated when conditions change over time, a reality much less common with ordinary instructions than legal rules. How should someone who has received such instructions react? Suppose the parent is actually away for some months, and the person caring for her children becomes aware that the price of one product has risen dramatically and another involved food that has been found to be somewhat dangerous to a child's health. Do the meaning of the instructions and faithful performance require adherence to the content of the instructions? Of course in modern times, it will almost certainly be possible to communicate with the parent about what should be done, but that was not always true. And we can imagine a parent who has become a prisoner of war, or is suffering an illness that prevents communication, or has actually died. If we ask what should the caregiver do, we can imagine a number of relevant factors. How comparatively expert are the caregiver and the parent about a subject? How flexible did each conceive the caregiver's duties in relation to the instructions? How strong and decisive are the reasons to depart from what the instructions literally mean? Connected to all this one might ask whether the instructions now mean what they originally did. If one understands that the parent's purpose was to have done what was good for the children, one might say the instructions no longer "mean" that the caregiver should purchase a food that is seriously dangerous. It may matter here how definite and severe that danger is. The caregiver might decide to stick with the specific instruction if the danger is modest and debatable.

Similar questions arise with legal standards, and, putting aside contracts between two persons still alive, the opportunity for quick and simple revisions does not exist. Officials have to decide how far original textual meaning and enactor intentions count when various changes in circumstances, including cultural values, suggest that adherence to specific terms would now be misguided.

What this reflection on informal instructions shows us is that given variations in expertness and in relations between the instructors and those instructed, we can imagine situations in which what constitutes "faithful performance" can differ with the same verbal instructions. We need also to understand that we can conceive of more than one "meaning," or that the determination of what really counts as "the meaning" rests on a judgment about desirable performance, which itself depends on multiple factors.

We lack an overall theoretical structure to tell us what meaning counts in all instances. An ordinary understanding of instructions depends both on context and shared assumptions of the speaker and listener. "Meaning" need not always correlate with best performance, and the relevant meaning may shift over time and may also depend on whether someone is deciding how to perform or is reviewing how someone else performed.

Many of these complexities are reflected in what counts as legally binding norms, and they may help explain that complicating elements of much legal interpretation are not unique to the law. On the other hand, the law, with its formality and official enforcement, is special in a number of ways. What one may conclude about some or all informal instructions does not tell us exactly how judges should act. One consideration here is determining relevant facts. If we say that speakers' intentions are a significant element for what instructions mean and what should be done for faithful performance, we might simply acknowledge that sometimes when we need to decide how to act, the crucial intentions of supervisors may be less than clear. We can live with these uncertainties. But in the law, at some point, a final decision may need to be made. This could be a reason to accord actual intentions less importance than in informal relations, since discerning those intentions can often be difficult for judges. Of course, a crucial point here is that discerning governing intentions of a multi-member body can often be impossible, and if one focuses on application to a particular situation, no relevant shared intention may be present. I do think intentions properly play a role in statutory and constitutional interpretation, but they are less dominant than the role they play with respect to informal instructions given by single individuals.

This review of informal instructions should give us some reassurance that the complexities and disputes concerning legal interpretation are not the product of judges and legal scholars failing to consider things in a simple and fair way. This chapter supports a number of conclusions of earlier ones. For example, in some particular circumstances, the relevant meaning and applications of legal standards are clear. We can say for these either that "interpretation is clear" or "interpretation is unnecessary," depending on how broadly we conceive the term "interpretation."

VI. CONCLUSION

We have seen in this chapter how other forms of interpretation and general theories can provide some insight into what is involved in legal interpretation and what is feasible or impossible. On occasion, these perspectives may help to suggest why one approach is better than an alternative. More broadly, this study gives us a reassurance that many of the complexities and disputes within law are not limited to that domain, but rather reflect complications that are simply aspects of our lives on earth and our understanding of fellow humans. We cannot find from theories outside the law clear answers to the delicate interpretive questions that face judges and other officials deciding what the law requires in debatable instances.

Conclusion

The chapters of this book have explored various themes, but they all relate to a dominant message. Although what the law requires is often obvious, when it comes down to difficult cases, we have no simple and straightforward way that judges do decide, and should decide, what is required. Categorizations do not provide obvious answers in these situations. All of these considerations resemble many aspects of our lives. We have many illustrations of behaviors that are definitely right or definitely wrong, but we also face situations in which we are not sure what we should do, and we lack a simple technique to determine the best response. I have made recommendations about particular practices that I hope readers have considered, but one can reject many of these and still accept the basic theme.

Chapter 1 explores the relation of text and intent. Although we have plausible arguments that the emphasis should be on the text, and that judges lack the capacity to make various assessments of intent, nevertheless we need to understand that readers and listeners typically understand instructions in terms of what they take their instructors to intend. This means we have no clear division between the two. And, as the chapter explores, exactly what should count for understanding with regard to the crucial text and the relevant intentions present nuances that lack clear answers.

Chapter 2 deals with changes in time and the role of fundamental values. Especially when an authoritative document is very hard to amend, as is the U.S. Constitution, and crucial values change over time, such as the status of women in relation to men, and the appropriateness of gay sexual relations and married couples, the reasons are very powerful to treat the application of open-ended provisions such as the equal protection clause in a flexible way.

Chapter 3 examines a few categorizations, such as "interpretation," "faithful agent," and "meaning." It attempts to show why these should not be taken as providing clear answers to debatable cases.

Chapter 4, without examining the subject in great depth, looks at how some of the issues are dealt with in other countries. We can see some significant variations based on cultures and political structures, but we can also recognize that what are often taken as flaws or problems in American practices also exist elsewhere. This suggests that many of these are unavoidable, and that we should accept them.

The final chapter looks at interpretation in other disciplines. These disciplines can provide some insights into, and reveal comparisons with, legal interpretation; but they do not tell us much about how judges should perform in difficult cases.

The book as a whole deals with a wide range of legal sources, including wills, contracts, trusts, statutes, administrative regulations, constitutions, and the common law. It recognizes that significant differences in these areas lead to different forms of interpretation, some of which are a good bit simpler than others. A common question among many of these topics is how much weight precedents should carry, and how much deference judges should afford to the positions of other officials who have made initial determinations about the law's application. Even when we address all these variations, we come back to the basic thesis that for debatable cases, no straightforward technique or categorization does or should provide a simple answer. My hope is that all this will help non-lawyer readers, and lawyers whose work and interest lie elsewhere, to understand why complexities and controversies do not mean our system is fundamentally defective.

NOTES

CHAPTER 1

1. Michael S. Schmidt, *Comey Memo Says Trump Asked Him to End Flynn Investigation*, N.Y. Times (May 16, 2017), https://www.nytimes.com/2017/05/16/us/politics/james-comey-trump-flynn-russia-investigation.html.
2. *See* 1–5 Harrison on Wills & Administration for Virginia & West Virginia § 5.03 (Charlottesville: Michie Co. 2017). In respect to joint wills and mutual wills, see 1 Jeffrey A. Schoenblum, Page on the Law of Wills § 11.1 (Newark: LexisNexis Matthew Bender 2017).
3. 494 U.S. 872 (1990).
4. 42 U.S.C. §§ 2000bb-1 to 2000bb-4 (1994).
5. On will substitutes, see John Langbein, *Substantial Compliance with the Wills Act*, 88 Harv. L. Rev. 489, 503–509 (1975) and *The Nonprobate Revolution and the Future of the Law of Succession*, 97 Harv. L. Rev. 1108 (1984); Nathaniel W. Schwickerath, *Public Policy and the Probate Pariah: Confusion in the Law of Will Substitutes*, 48 Drake L. Rev. 769 (2000).
6. *See* Devin Looijen, *Time for a Change: The Schema of Contract in the Digital Era*, 8 J. Telecomm. & High Tech. L. 547, 557–58, 564–65 (2010).
7. Estate of Taff, 133 Cal. Rptr. 737 (Ct. App. 1976).
8. In re Dorson's Estate, 196 N.Y.S.2d 344 (Sur. 1959).
9. In re Estate of Gibbs, 111 N.W.2d 413 (1961).
10. In re Rowland, [1963] Ch. 1 (Eng. C. A.).
11. Conceivably general usage in Great Britain at the time of Dr. Rowland's will was much narrower than what I take as general usage now, but, partly because I was a student at Oxford from 1958 to 1960, I do not believe that was so.
12. *See* U.C.C. § 2–202 on Final Written Expression: Parol or Extrinsic Evidence (Am. Law Inst. & Unif. Law Comm'n 2012); United Nations Convention on Contracts for the International Sale of Goods, 19 I.L.M. 668, 673 (1980).
13. Spaulding v. Morse, 76 N.E.2d 137, 138 (Sup. Jud. Ct. Mass. 1947).
14. Raffles v. Wichehaus, 159 Eng. Rep. 375 (Ex. 1864).
15. E. Allan Farnsworth, "*Meaning" in the Law of Contracts*, 76 Yale L.J. 939, 950 (1967) (quoting Restatement (First) of Contracts § 230 (Am. Law Inst. 1932)).
16. Restatement (Second) of Contracts § 201 (2)(a)(b) (Am. Law Inst.1981).

17. Alaska S.S. Co. v. United States, 290 U.S. 256 (1933).
18. 490 U.S. 504 (1989).
19. 508 U.S. 223 (1993).
20. 143 U.S. 457 (1892).
21. *See supra* text accompanying note 4.
22. *See* RONALD DWORKIN, A MATTER OF PRINCIPLE 322 (Cambridge, MA: Harvard University Press 1985); Paul Brest, *The Misconceived Quest for the Original Understanding*, 60 B.U. L. REV. 204, 209–13 (1980).
23. *See* JUSTICE ANTONIN SCALIA, A MATTER OF INTERPRETATION: FEDERAL COURTS AND THE LAW 18–23 (Princeton: Princeton University Press 1996) (critiquing *Church of the Holy Trinity, supra* note 20).
24. For a more detailed account, see KENT GREENAWALT, INTERPRETING THE CONSTITUTION 49–50 (New York: Oxford University Press 2015).
25. 384 U.S. 436 (1966).
26. Peter L. Strauss has provided a clear and detailed account of this subject in ADMINISTRATIVE JUSTICE IN THE UNITED STATES (3d ed. Durham: Carolina Academic Press 2016).
27. On the role and function of administrative adjudications, see Charles M. Koch, Jr., *Policymaking by the Administrative Judiciary*, ALA. L. REV. 693 (2005), and Christopher B. McNeil, *Critical Factors of Adjudication: Language and the Adjudicative Process in Executive and Judicial Branch Decisions*, 23 J. NAT'L ASS'N ADMIN. L. JUDGES 411 (2003).
28. *See* Peter L. Strauss, *The Trump Transition and American Administrative Law* (forthcoming).
29. 5 U.S.C. §§ 551–59, 701–06 (1946).
30. *See* Aditya Bamzai, *The "Administrative Process" in the 1940s Court: A Study in Intellectual and Jurisprudential History* (forthcoming).
31. On how courts have responded to this, see STRAUSS, *supra* note 26, at 426.
32. N.L.R.B. v. Hearst Publications, Inc., 322 U.S. 111, 130 (1944).
33. STRAUSS, *supra* note 26, at 501.
34. 467 U.S. 837, 843 (1984).
35. *See* Philip Hamburger, *Chevron Bias*, 84 GEO. WASH. L. REV. 1187 (2016).
36. *See* STRAUSS, *supra* note 26, at 51, 495–96.
37. Lochner v. New York, 198 U.S. 45 (1905).
38. *See* Dana Berliner, *The Federal Rational Basis Test—Fact and Fiction*, 14 GEO. J.L. & PUB. POL'Y 373 (2016).
39. 304 U.S. 144 (1938).
40. 348 U.S. 483 (1955).
41. FCC v. Beach Commc'ns, 508 U.S. 307, 313 (1993).
42. *See, e.g.*, Berliner, *supra* note 38.
43. U.S. CONST. amend. V.
44. U.S. CONST. amend. XIV, § 1.
45. *See* John O. McGinnis, *Reforming Constitutional Review of State Economic Legislation*, 14 GEO. J.L. & PUB. POL'Y 517, 527–35 (2016).

CHAPTER 2

1. *See* U. Prob. C. § 2–202, Elective Share (National Conference of Commissioners on Uniform State Laws 1982); Raymond C. O'Brien, *Integrating Marital Property into a Spouse's Elective Share*, 59 Cath. U. L. Rev. 617, 640 (2010).
2. Notably, children born after a will is written or adopted are included unless explicitly excluded. *See* U. Prob. C. § 2–302, Omitted Children (National Conference of Commissioners on Uniform State Laws 1982).
3. 115 N.Y. 506, 22 N.E. 188 (1889).
4. *See* Taylor v. Caldwell, [1863] Queen's Bench, 3 Best S. 826 (opinion of Justice Blackburn).
5. Krell v. Henry, 2 K.B. 740 (1903).
6. Restatement (Second) of Contracts § 265 (Am. Law Inst. 1982).
7. 444 A. 2d 659, 660 (Pa. Sup. Ct. 1982).
8. First Church in Somerville (Unitarian) v. Attorney Gen., 375 Mass. 332 N.E. 2d 1226 (Mass. 1978).
9. *Id.* at 334.
10. Mercury Bay Boating Club v. San Diego Yacht Club, 76 N.Y. 256 (1990).
11. Evans v. Abney, 396 U.S. 435 (1970).
12. 477 A.2d 1066 (Del. 1984).
13. 398 U.S. 333 (1970).
14. *Id.* at 344–54 (J. Harlan, concurring in judgment).
15. 242 US 470 (1917).
16. 392 U.S. 409 (1968).
17. 467 U.S. 837 (1984).
18. Green v. Bock Laundry Mach. Co., 490 U.S. 504 (1989).
19. I have written briefly on this topic. *See Probabilities, Perceptions, Consequences and "Discrimination": One Puzzle about Controversial "Stop and Frisk"*, 12 Ohio St. J. Crim. L. 181 (2014).
20. U.S. Const. amend II.
21. 554 U.S. 570, 574–75 (2008).
22. 384 U.S. 436 (1966).
23. *See* Peter Linzer, *The Meaning of Certiorari Denials*, 79 Colum. L. Rev. 1227 (1979); Kathryn A. Watts, *Constraining Certiorari Using Administrative Law Principles*, 160 U. Pa. L. Rev. 1, 18–19, 22 (2011); Linda R. Cohen & Matthew L. Spitzer, *Judicial Deference to Agency Action: A Rational Choice Theory and an Empirical Test*, 69 S. Cal. L. Rev. 431, 438 (1996).
24. 494 U.S. 872 (1990).
25. 384 U.S. 436 (1966).
26. 136 Me. 347, 9 A. 2d 657 (1939).
27. *Id.* at 658.
28. *Id.*

CHAPTER 3

1. In re Estate of Gibbs, 111 N.W.2d 413 (Wis. 1961).
2. Estate of Taff, 133 Cal. Rptr. 737 (Ct. App. 1976).

3. In re Rowland, [1963] Ch. 1 (Eng. C.A.).
4. On how far the Common Law, Restatement, and Uniform Probate Code allow revision of terms, see Adam J. Hirsch, *Testation and the Mind*, 72 WASH. & LEE L. REV. 285, 315–17 (2017).
5. Krell v. Henry, 2 K.B. 740 (1903).
6. Spaulding v. Morse, 76 N.E. 2d 137, 138 (Sup. Jud. Ct. Mass. 1947).
7. Steuart v. McChesney, 444 A. 2d 659 (Pa. Sup. Ct. 1982).
8. United States v. Seeger, 360 U.S. 163 (1965); Welsh v. United States, 398 U.S. 333 (1970).
9. Green v. Bock Laundry Mach. Co., 490 U.S. 504 (1989).
10. Riggs v. Palmer, 115 N.Y. 506, 22 N.E. 188 (1889).
11. Smith v. United States, 508 U.S. 223 (1993).
12. Obergefell v. Hodges, 135 S. Ct. 2584 (2015).
13. *See* Mark Greenberg, *The Moral Impact Theory of Law*, 123 YALE L.J. 1288 (2014); Mark Greenberg, *What Makes a Method of Legal Interpretation Correct? Legal Standards vs. Fundamental Determinants*, 130 HARV. L. REV. F. 105 (2017).

CHAPTER 4

1. Green v. Bock Laundry Mach. Co., 490 U.S. 504 (1989).
2. 4 Burr. 2303, 98 Eng. Rep. R. 201 (K.B. 1769).
3. [1993] 1 All E.R. 42 (H.L. 1992).
4. Holger Fleischer, *Comparative Approaches to the Use of Legislative History in Statutory Interpretation*, 60 AM. J. COMP. L. 401, 404–12 (2012).
5. *Id.* at 412–14.
6. *Id.* at 414–15.
7. The recent article analyzing this describes various critiques of the German practice.
8. See generally Richard Ekins & Jeffrey Goldsworthy, *The Reality and Indispensability of Legislative Intentions*, 26 SYDNEY L. REV. 30 (2013).
9. See Erin Daly, *Idealists, Pragmatists, and Textualists: Judging Electoral Districts in America, Canada, and Australia,* 21 B.C. INT'L & COMP. L. REV. 261, 349–51 (1998).
10. Lacey v. Attorney General (Qld) (2011) 242 (IR 573, 591–92).
11. ELMER A. DRIEDGER, THE CONSTRUCTION OF STATUTES (1st ed. Toronto: Butterworths 1974).
12. ELMER A. DRIEDGER, THE CONSTRUCTION OF STATUTES 8 (2d ed. Toronto: Butterworths 1983).
13. [1998] 1 S.C.R. 27.
14. Ruth Sullivan, *Statutory Interpretation in the Supreme Court of Canada*, 30 OTTAWA L. REV. 175 (1999).
15. *Id.* at 192.
16. [1991] 3 S.C.R. 72.
17. Sullivan, *supra* note 14, at 224.
18. *See* Hon. Justice Michael Kirby, Towards a Grand Theory of Interpretation, The Case of Statutes and Contracts, Joint Conference of Clarity and Statute Law at Cambridge University (July 13, 2002).

19. Shawn J. Bayern, *The Nature and Timing of Contract Formation*, *in* COMPARATIVE CONTRACT LAW: BRITISH AND AMERICAN PERSPECTIVES 89 (Larry A. DiMatteo & Martin Hogg eds., New York: Oxford University Press 2016).
20. Mark P. Gergen, *The Right to Perform after Repudiation and Recover the Contract Price in Anglo-American Law*, *in* COMPARATIVE CONTRACT LAW: BRITISH AND AMERICAN PERSPECTIVES, *supra note* 19, at 330.
21. *See* Attorney General of Belize v. Belize Telecom Ltd. [2009] UKPC 10.
22. Marks & Spencer plc v. BNP Paribas Services [2015] UKSC 72.
23. Bank of Credit and Commerce International SA (in liquidation) v. Ali, 2001 UKHL 8.
24. Catherine Mitchell, *Interpreting Commercial Contracts: The Policing Role of Context in English Law*, *in* COMPARATIVE CONTRACT LAW: BRITISH AND AMERICAN PERSPECTIVES, *supra* note 19, at 231.
25. *Id.* at 234.
26. *See* Qi Zhou & Larry A. DiMatteo, *Three Sales Laws and the Common Law of Contracts*, *in* COMPARATIVE CONTRACT LAW: BRITISH AND AMERICAN PERSPECTIVES, *supra* note 19, at 358–59.
27. *See* Catherine Mitchell, *Reply to Blake D. Morant, "Contractual Interpretation in the Commercial Context*," *in* COMPARATIVE CONTRACT LAW: BRITISH AND AMERICAN PERSPECTIVES, *supra* note 19, at 288–89.
28. Hill v. Gateway 2000, Inc., 105 F.3d 1147 (7th Cir. 1997); Klocek v. Gateway, Inc., 104 F. Supp. 2d 1332 (D. Kan. 2000).
29. Aditi Bagchi, *At the Limits of Adjudication: Standard Terms in Consumer Contracts*, *in* COMPARATIVE CONTRACT LAW: BRITISH AND AMERICAN PERSPECTIVES, *supra* note 19, at 447.
30. Lord Hodge, *Can Judges Use Business Common Sense in Interpreting Contracts?*, *in* COMPARATIVE CONTRACT LAW: BRITISH AND AMERICAN PERSPECTIVES, *supra* note 19, at 281.
31. Mark P. Gergen, *The Right to Perform after Repudiation and Recover the Contract Price in Anglo-American Law*, *in* COMPARATIVE CONTRACT LAW: BRITISH AND AMERICAN PERSPECTIVES, *supra* note 19, at 332.
32. THEOBALD ON WILLS § C, ch. 13 (18th ed. London: Sweet & Maxweel Ltd. 2016).
33. *See id.* § 13–008.
34. *Id.* § 13–023.
35. *Id.* § 13–021.
36. *Id.* § 13–028.
37. Printz v. United States, 521 U.S. 898, 921, n.11 (1997).
38. *See* Sujit Choudhry, *Globalization in Search of Justification: Toward a Theory of Comparative Constitutional Interpretation*, 74 IND. L.J. 819 (1999).
39. Mark Tushnet, *The Possibilities of Comparative Constitutional Law*, 108 YALE L.J. 1225, 1270 (1999).
40. For a comparison of Canada and the United States, see Choudhry, *supra* note 38, at 886–87 (1999).

41. *See* Janet Kentridge & Derek Spitz, *Interpretation*, *in* the CONSTITUTIONAL LAW OF SOUTH AFRICA (Matthew Chaskalon, Janet Kentridge, Jonathan Klaaren, Gilbert Marcus, Derek Spitz, Stuart Woolman eds., Kenwyn: Juta & Company Ltd. 1999).
42. On those countries, see Yvonne Tew, *Originalism at Home and Abroad*, 52 COLUM. J. TRANSN'L L. 780, 800–29 (2014).
43. *See* Richard Albert, *American Exceptionalism in Constitutional Interpretation*, 69 ARK. L. REV. 216, 232–42 (2016).
44. *Id.* at 242–46.
45. *Id.* at 246
46. *Id.* at 225–27.
47. *See* Donald S. Lark, PRINCIPLES OF CONSTITUTIONAL DESIGN 154–70 (New York: Cambridge University Press 2006).
48. Edward J. Eberle, *Human Dignity, Privacy, and Personality in German and American Constitutional Law*, 1997 UTAH L. REV. 963, 969–71 (1997).
49. Singh v Commonwealth (2004) 209 ALR 355 (opinion of McHugh, J).
50. Australian National Airways Pty Ltd v. Commonwealth (1945) 71 CLR 29, at 81 (opinion of Dixon, J.).
51. *See* Kentridge and Spitz, *supra* note 41.
52. *See* Matthew J. Moore, *Revisiting Constitutional Interpretation: A Comparative Perspective on the American Debates*, *in* 28 STUDIES IN LAW, POLITICS, AND SOCIETY 3, 8–13 (Austin Sarat & Patricia Ewick eds., Bingley, UK: Emerald Group Publishing Limited, 2003).
53. *See* Tew, *supra* note 42.
54. *Id.* at 803.
55. *Id.* at 817.
56. *Id.* at 820.

CHAPTER 5

1. Two scholars who draw on such a comparison have been Sanford Levinson, "*The Constitution" in American Civil Religion*, 1979 SUP. CT. REV. 123 (1979), and Ronald Garet, *Comparative Normative Hermeneutics: Scripture, Literature, Constitution*, 58 S.C. L. REV. 35 (1985).
2. *See* ELAINE PAGELS, THE GNOSTIC GOSPELS (New York: Random House 1979); BEYOND BELIEF (New York: Random House 2003).
3. For two different positions on Jewish law, and particularly the inclusion of dissenting views in the Talmud, see Suzanne Last Stone, *In Pursuit of the Counter-Text: The Turn to the Jewish Legal Model in Contemporary American Legal Theory*, 106 HARV. L. REV. 813 (1993); Robert M. Cover, *Obligation: A Jewish Jurisprudence of the Social Order*, 5 J.L. & RELIGION 65 (1987).
4. See 1 MENACHEM ELON, JEWISH LAW: HISTORY SOURCES, PRINCIPLES 339–40 (Philadelphia: Jewish Publication Society 1999).
5. IMRAN AHSAN NYAZEE, THEORIES OF ISLAMIC LAW 55, 131–33 (Islamabad: Islamabad International Institute of Islamic Thought 1994).
6. *Augustine, Confessions*, ch. 18, *as reprinted in* BARRIE A. WILSON, ABOUT INTERPRETATION 69, 71 (New York: Peter Lang 1988).

7. *See, e.g.*, Terry Eagleton, Literary Theory: An Introduction 1–16 (2d. ed. Minneapolis: University of Minnesota Press 1996).
8. *See* Ronald Dworkin, *Law as Interpretation*, 60 Tex. L. Rev. 527 (1982).
9. *See, e.g.*, Wolfgang Iser, The Implied Reader: Patterns of Communication in Prose Fiction from Bunyan to Beckett (Baltimore: Johns Hopkins University Press 1974).
10. Martha Nussbaum, Poetic Justice 1–52 (Boston: Beacon Press 1995).
11. *See, e.g.*, Paul Grice, *Meaning*, 66 Phil. Rev. 377 (1957); Studies in the Way of Words 290–97 (Cambridge, MA: Harvard University Press, 1989).
12. *See supra* Chapter 1 note 9.
13. *See supra* Chapter 1 note 20.
14. One influential theory is that of Hans-Georg Gadamer, developed most fully in Truth and Method (2d rev. ed.) (New York: Crossroad Publishing 1989).
15. *See id.*
16. Clifford Geertz, *Deep Play, Notes on the Balinese Cockfight*, *in* Interpretation and Social Science: A Second Look 195–240 (Paul Rabinow & William M. Sullivan eds.) (Berkeley: University of California Press, 1987).

INDEX

The manufacturer's authorised representative in the EU for product
safety is Oxford University Press España S.A. of El Parque Empresarial
San Fernando de Henares, Avenida de Castilla, 2 - 28830 Madrid
(www.oup.es/en or product.safety@oup.com). OUP España S.A. also acts
as importer into Spain of products made by the manufacturer.
Printed and bound by CPI Group (UK) Ltd, Croydon, CR0 4YY
14/09/2026
02216295-0006